P9-DFI-184

JOHN HAY WHITNEY FOUNDATION

Volume I

JOHN HAY WHITNEY FOUNDATION

A Report of the First Twenty-five Years

Volume I

THE OPPORTUNITY FELLOWS

THE WHITNEY-FULBRIGHT PROFESSORS

THE WHITNEY VISITING PROFESSORS

By
Esther Raushenbush

JOHN HAY WHITNEY FOUNDATION · NEW YORK · 1972

Contents

Foreword

As early as 1940 John Hay Whitney began discussing with his associates, particularly William H. Jackson, the establishment of a charitable foundation. During the war years these conversations were continued sporadically; and in the fall of 1945, after Mr. Whitney's return from military service, a series of meetings began, based on his decision to establish such an institution. Originally, consideration was given to the needs of blacks and to social welfare in general. Shortly thereafter interest shifted to the field of general education, particularly to programs designed to help educate high school and other public school students through the use of radio, motion pictures, and other media which had proved effective for mass education. In October 1945 President Edmund E. Day of Cornell University suggested that Mr. Whitney consult with Beardsley Ruml, among others, on possible Foundation programs. Stemming from these conversations with Mr. Ruml, Mr. Whitney met Dr. Edwin R. Embree, at that time the executive director of the Rosenwald Fund and soon to become the first consultant of the Greenwood Foundation, which became at a later date the John Hay Whitney Foundation.

Mr. Ruml emphasized that it was imperative that the programs of a small foundation utilize what he called "leverage." He stressed the fact that not only was this factor essential but also that the degree of leverage achievable should be carefully examined before any specific program was undertaken. Applications of this principle will be apparent throughout these two volumes, which review the history of the Foundation during its first twenty-five years of operation. During these formative years another person frequently consulted because of her wide familiarity with the problems under discussion was Mrs. Anna M. Rosenberg.

After many more conferences with many individuals, the Foundation was incorporated in late 1946 under the Non-Profit Membership Corporations Law of the State of New York with an initial gift of $200,000 from the founder. The first meeting of its trustees—Mr. and Mrs. Whitney and Mr. Jackson—who had been closely joined in all the deliberations even during the war years, was held on December 16, 1946. Robert Blum was elected secretary of the Foundation and acted as its first but unofficial director.

During the first year of its existence Mr. Blum continued conversation with individuals in the fields of education and philanthropy all over the United States, searching for desirable permanent fields of activity for the Foundation. It was not until January 1947 that the trustees approved its first major grant, made to the National Planning Association, Washington, D.C., toward the support of a series of inquiries into the factors inhibiting strikes under collective bargaining. This series of studies was published in booklet form and distributed widely throughout the United States under the collective title *Causes of Industrial Peace.* Ten of the studies supported by the Foundation appeared between 1947 and 1952. While continuing the search for a general field of activity, an application was received from Dr. Charles S. Johnson, director of the Department of Social Sciences, and president-elect of Fisk University, for a grant to support ten fellowships over a three-year period to Negro graduate students in the social sciences at Fisk University. Under Dr. Johnson's leadership, Fisk had developed one of the most important centers for the study of Negro problems. On April 30, 1947, this grant was made.

The contact with Dr. Johnson proved to be of great importance to the Foundation, as he became, after the death of Dr. Embree, its second consultant. During Dr. Johnson's period as a consultant the major programs of the Foundation were initiated and developed. It was also through Dr. Johnson that the Foundation's third consultant, Dr. Harry S. Carman, was introduced to the Foundation.

In June 1947, coincident with Mr. Blum's resignation as secretary of the Foundation, the trustees decided to stop the search for special programs and to limit activity to making grants to other charitable or tax-exempt organizations. This activity remained the Foundation's approach until the spring of 1949 when Mr. Whitney made a $1,000,000 gift to the Foundation, and the trustees resumed the search for specific fields to support. As Mr. Blum's successor and to administer its operation, Samuel C. Park, Jr., was elected secretary-treasurer and later, in 1953, vice president.

After the liquidation of the Rosenwald Fund in 1949, the services of Dr. Embree became available; he was retained as consultant on a part-time basis by the Foundation. On September 1, 1949, he resumed the search to find permanent fields of activity for the Foundation. Largely because of his familiarity with the urgent need of Negro students for aid in carrying on graduate studies, on September 29, 1949, the trustees authorized the establishment of the Opportunity Fellowships Program for a five-year period, with an annual appropriation of $100,000. They also decided that other Foundation programs should be developed and supported by additional budgets aggregating $300,000 a year.

On November 7, 1949, a fourth trustee, Mr. Barklie McKee Henry, was elected to the board.

To determine the criteria and methods for selecting Opportunity Fellows, Dr. Embree on behalf of the trustees organized a two-day seminar, which was held in New York City in early December 1949. The Committee of Award was appointed, which served, with some continuing and some changing membership, throughout the life of the program.

On October 26, 1949, the Greenwood Foundation became the John Hay Whitney Foundation. Most unfortunately at this critical point in the Foundation's real beginning, Dr. Embree suddenly died on February 21, 1950. The Board membership was increased to seven; and Mrs. Rosenberg, Dr. Johnson, and Mr. Park were elected trustees on March 15,

1950. In June Dr. Johnson was officially designated consultant.

In February, March, and April the continuing active discussions among the trustees were influenced particularly by memoranda submitted by Dr. Johnson and Mr. Henry and accented by comments from President Whitney Griswold of Yale and other educators. In May 1950, the trustees decided that the major interest of the Foundation would lie in the general field of the humanities.

On Dr. Johnson's recommendation, the next program initiated by the Foundation was a series of three-year grants to five universities to permit them to establish the Embree Memorial Lectures.

At this early date enough interest had been aroused by the Opportunity Fellowships Program to stimulate a representative of the Kahn Family Fund of Dallas, Texas, to meet with representatives of the Foundation. Later the Kahn Fund agreed to provide up to six additional Opportunity Fellowships a year to be used specifically for Fellows selected from Texas.

Having determined that the interest of the Foundation was to be in the area of the humanities, the trustees in consultation with Dr. Johnson held, on February 16, 1951, a one-day seminar participated in directly and indirectly by some thirty individuals prominent in the field of education from all areas of the country, ranging from the Atlantic to the Pacific and the Canadian border to the Gulf of Mexico. It was hoped that their deliberations would yield major projects for the John Hay Whitney Foundation; and indeed the John Hay Fellowships grew out of this seminar as the Opportunity Fellowships had resulted from the meeting of December 1949.

The stories of the Opportunity Fellowships, the Whitney–Fulbright Professorships, and the Whitney Visiting Professors are told in Volume I; the John Hay Fellowships, in Volume II.

December 1, 1971   S. C. P.

Introduction

There has never been a time in our history when the dislocations in our society—a more complex society than has ever existed on earth—were more visible, or cried out more earnestly for intelligence, will, and effort to resolve them. It becomes clearer every day that they will never be resolved without a deeply engaged intention to confront them. And it is difficult, now, to consider any sustained human action without considering, too, how such action might affect the resolution of our problems.

The programs of the John Hay Whitney Foundation cannot cure our ills. But from its beginning this Foundation has had as its ruling purpose the creation of programs directed toward the enlargement of life for those who took part in them, and for others whose lives touched theirs. A look back over twenty-five years gives the image of an extraordinarily consistent adherence to this major purpose.

The activities of the Foundation have demonstrated a faith in the possibilities of education. Its support of educational programs during the twenty-five years has gone to a variety of people and a variety of educational enterprises; but it has all had a common direction.

The two volumes now being published, which review the programs of the Foundation from its beginnings, demonstrate its interest in humanistic studies and in broadly humanistic education. The Foundation came into existence right after World War II. Its purposes were defined and its programs developed during that convulsive postwar period when, one war scarcely over, there was intense concern with the possibilities of another—years during which Sputnik, and scientific discoveries generally, led to an enormous emphasis on scientific education—a time when our attention, as citizens and educators, was less on human values and more on the values of science and on international and domestic political power struggles.

The concern with a humanistic view of the world and with the values of a humanistic education, which has dominated the activities of the Foundation, was a direct outgrowth of a concern about individuals, about American education, and about the need for diverse people to understand each other which Mr. Whitney brought back with him from his experiences in World War II. He points to these experiences in describing how he decided to create the Foundation. He was taken prisoner in 1944, when on a tour of observation as staff officer for Lieutenant General Ira Eaker, commander of the Allied Air Forces in the Mediterranean, after the landings in southern France. He escaped after some weeks with eleven other prisoners from a boxcar of a moving train that was taking them to Germany. It was the conversation of his fellow prisoners that turned Mr. Whitney's attention to the problems of American education.

What impressed him deeply, in long conversations with his fellow prisoners, was that he rarely encountered among them one who was able or willing to say what he was fighting for—what moral issues were involved in the struggle with Nazism. This, he concluded, was a failure, not of these individuals but of education; and he determined then that he would do what he could to encourage the kind of education that was concerned with moral and social values.

Shortly after Mr. Whitney returned to civilian life he established the John Hay Whitney Foundation. Samuel C. Park, Jr., an officer of the Foundation from the beginning, has written an account of its establishment in the foreword to this volume. Mr. Whitney's first concern was for men and women whose economic, racial, or educational background made them unequal competitors for a liberal education, and out of this concern grew the Opportunity Fellowships described in this volume.

ESTABLISHING PROGRAMS

THE OPPORTUNITY FELLOWS

The earliest project was the Opportunity Fellowship Program; between 1950 and 1971, 953 individuals were awarded fellowships for graduate or professional study, and study in the arts. The recipients were principally American Indians, blacks, Mexican Americans, impoverished mountain whites, Puerto Ricans, students from the Pacific Island Trust Territories, and, in the earlier years of the program, Japanese and Chinese living in this country. The recipients of Opportunity Fellowships were selected because they were able people who encountered unusual barriers to professional and graduate education by the condition of their lives. The individuals selected were principally people interested in the study of the humanities, including the social sciences, and in professions significantly concerned with human problems and human values. Few fellowships were granted to individuals engaged in pure research in science—the fields most generously supported by government and industry at the time the fellowships were established.

THE WHITNEY–FULBRIGHT PROFESSORS

A Whitney Foundation program provided funds between 1951 and 1965 to pay the salaries of forty-eight foreign professors to teach American undergraduates. During the '50s the Fulbright Act provided travel funds for foreign scholars to spend a year in the colleges and universities of this country. A large part of the travel money went to scholars who came here to do research and to work with graduate students in the universities—these were the men whom the universities were most willing to appoint to posts here. The salary funds the Whitney Foundation made available were for the teaching of undergraduates, preferably in undergraduate colleges and preferably in small colleges or universities that might not otherwise have the money to attract these scholars who could be (and were) very important additions to education in this country.

From the Whitney–Fulbright foreign professors' project grew the Whitney–Fulbright Orientation Program. For twelve years, from 1954 through 1965, the Foundation financed and planned, along with the federal government, an annual orientation conference to which scholars coming to the United States to teach undergraduates were invited for a week of discussion with their American counterparts, as a way of being introduced to American undergraduate education.

THE WHITNEY VISITING PROFESSORS

In 1952, the Foundation established the Whitney Visiting Professors in the humanities. A writer describing Mr. Whitney's Foundation career points out that the John Hay and Opportunity Fellowship programs were designed by professional educators called on by Mr. Whitney, but that the plan for the Visiting Professors was "pure Whitney."

An associate described its genesis. It seems that in a conversation with friends mention was made of the fact that a much-admired professor had reached the mandatory retirement age at his university and would end his teaching career at the close of that academic year. Dismayed by this Mr. Whitney promptly decided some way must be found to enable such men to continue to use their talents—and in some place where they were seriously needed. Plans took shape, and the following year the Whitney Visiting Professorships, for retiring professors, was established. The program provided for appointment of distinguished teachers to undergraduate colleges for one year after their retirement. Like the Whitney–Fulbright Professors, these men and women were appointed to colleges that could not otherwise afford their services, and gave new and unexpected opportunities to students in such colleges to study with people who had been distinguished teachers in distinguished universities. The program led to the establishment of the Retired Professors Registry, which, along with the program itself, is described in this volume.

THE JOHN HAY FELLOWS

Finally, the largest and the most fully designed and developed of the Foundation programs, the John Hay Fellowships, was created in 1952. It was funded by the Whitney Foundation until 1959. At that time the Ford Foundation undertook to support this program, under the aegis of the Whitney Foundation, until 1966. The story of the interest and participation of the Ford Foundation is told in Chapter 6 of *The John Hay Fellows*, Volume II in this account of the Whitney Foundation programs.

In the fourteen years of its existence over two thousand high school teachers and administrators had had the experience of a year or a summer or both of planned university study, mainly in the humanities and the social sciences. This program developed from the discussions of a group of scholars whom Mr. Whitney invited to a seminar to discuss ways of encouraging education in the humanities in a time when great energy, large sums of money, and strong convictions were shaping intense study and research in science to a degree never known before. The story of this seminar, and of the creation of the John Hay Fellowships for high school teachers which grew out of it, is told in the second chapter of *The John Hay Fellows*.[1] That book is an account of an intellectual and personal experience of great importance for those who became students in the program, and those who taught in it. It brought a special kind of life into the schools to which the participants returned, and the universities in which they studied.

THE ENDURING PURPOSE

It should be noticed here that the interest of the Foundation in talented individuals whose promise and performance as high school teachers were to be enhanced by a year of study in a great university; in able individuals whose opportunities for professional development were limited because of economic, cultural, or racial barriers; in educators from abroad who could bring their knowledge to American undergraduates; and in retired professors in the fields of the humanities, all had a consistent purpose. As will be seen in these two volumes, the programs were imaginatively and carefully designed to fulfill that purpose. They are the response to Mr.

1. A list of the participants in the 1951 seminar is found on p. xxiv.

Whitney's belief, beginning with his experience in the war, that education for humanistic ends needed to be improved in this country.

ANOTHER PART OF THE FOREST

That was in 1944. Two years later the first funds of the John Hay Whitney Foundation were made available. Twenty-five years have gone by. More than two thousand individuals have participated in long-range programs of the Foundation—have had a year or more of work or study with its support; nearly a thousand more have participated in the shorter programs—a summer institute for high school administrators and teachers, orientation sessions for foreign professors coming to this country to teach college undergraduates. During most of this time the interest of the Foundation in granting funds has been the individual development of the recipients; and the recipients were people with the intellectual and human qualities the Foundation was interested in fostering.

This has been the thrust of the Opportunity Fellowship program. The Foundation looked for people with high potential whose economic condition, personal life, and schooling had been barriers to an adequate chance to develop that potential; and since these barriers were most conspicuous and most impenetrable among racial minorities, most of the funds were used for individuals from those groups.

Similarly, for the first period of the John Hay Fellowships, the Foundation's effort was to find promising high school teachers, wherever they were, for whom a year of study in the humanities promised significant intellectual fulfillment, which, to be sure, would in turn affect their teaching. Also, the appointment of the retired professors to small colleges for a year was for the purpose of giving to the teacher, at the end of his teaching career, the chance to continue in a new situation where he was needed, and to his students the experience of associating with a distinguished teacher from another place. Teaching American undergraduates gave both the Fulbright professors from abroad, and the students they taught, new light on their own experience as teachers and students.

This emphasis on the intellectual and personal value to the

individuals who have participated in the programs continues to be important. But this is a different time; we are now in another part of the forest.

The past twenty-five years have given dramatic evidence of the failure in our national life to act in terms of those intellectual, moral, and social values that the work of the John Hay Whitney Foundation has sought to develop. But at the same time there has never been the sharp, articulate consciousness of that failure among as many people as there is now; nor so much awareness that the difficulties we face must be directly dealt with, not only by the concern for talented individuals but also by the improvement of our institutional life. It is not enough that able high school teachers improve their own teaching and their personal and intellectual lives; it is not enough that a talented black student be given an opportunity to achieve a satisfactory professional life, or that a Mexican American find it possible with fellowship help to escape the restrictions of life in the barrio and make his way to what we have called the mainstream of American life. Always, any effort to deal with our ills must work through individual people; but if they, and the country as a whole, are to deal with our ills effectively, our concern must go beyond these individuals to consider how a significant impact can be made on the institutions which in the end determine what this nation will become.

For this reason, the new programs of the Whitney Foundation, inspired by exactly the intellectual, moral, and social convictions which have lain behind all its work, continue to be concerned with people; but now the Foundation is concerned with people who are committed to making our institutions work better for the people they serve. Making them work better is a large order; and, to repeat, it is obvious that the Whitney Foundation cannot cure the society's ills. But it can help, by supporting people and programs that are dedicated to the effort. The next period of its activities will see them directed toward aiding the efforts of individuals and groups concerned with specific programs for the improvement of education and public affairs.

This orientation is not altogether new. The second stage of

the John Hay Fellowship Program, under the imaginative direction of Charles Keller, went beyond support for individual teachers, to support for individuals clustered within certain school systems that were trying to improve the study of the humanities and the social sciences in the high schools. Moreover, the summer institutes—which brought together superintendents, principals, and teachers from the same school system—tended to improve the system directly, as well as indirectly, through the effect of the experience on the individual. The impact of any program is hard to assess; but the story of the increased impact when the people supported are concerned directly with the improvement of the system as well as with their own professional lives, is a persuasive one—as the activities of the men and women who were John Hay Fellows and their effect on the schools from which they came, especially in the last seven years of the program, indicated.

In the case of the Opportunity Fellowships, no requirements, no priorities even, were stated about the use that the fellowship holder should make of his education for the future; but a review of the directions taken by them in their later careers gives a picture of how the needs visible in the 1950s and 1960s gave direction to the lives and work of the men and women selected for support in those decades. We know now that the issue is not whether Fellows who are Mexican Americans or Indians or blacks will work "among their people" or "in the society as a whole." Surely we have learned something in the past few years of education, action protest, legislation—learned from our failures in these areas as well as from such success as there has been. We have learned at least that the dislocations in the lives of the poor and the powerless are not *their* problems but problems the whole society has created and must solve. If the talented people who come from that part of the society most subject to the dislocations are indeed to deal with our ills, whether in education, in public service, or in any other aspect of the social structure, it will be as the ills of the whole society, not peculiar to the problem of any particular ethnic group.

This brings us back to the interest of the John Hay Whitney Foundation in the humanities. At a conference in September 1970 of men and women who have held Opportunity Fellowships (a discussion of what should be the concerns of the Foundation for the time immediately ahead) Ernesto Galarza said, "What we must deal with in these times is the strength which the inhumanities have shown in our society—we must turn to them, and must plan courses of action that will help to loosen their grip on us all."

This is no mere play on words. The values that, at the beginning of the life of this Foundation were defined as a guide to its purposes—"the insistent observation that will finally count in the preservation of the Humanities will be, beyond anything else, the humanistic attitude itself" and that "people matter more than things"—were themselves a commitment to find ways of overcoming the conditions of our life and to encourage men and women in those engagements that will help us all in the effort to overcome them.

For this reason the John Hay Whitney Foundation is planning, for the coming years, to support team projects: groups of men and women who will seek ways of overcoming particular effects of the "inhumanities" in our lives; to finance independent projects that will give men and women the opportunity to study and seek ways of dealing with dislocations in our schools and our other social institutions as they are demonstrated in particular places and under particular conditions; and to encourage such other activities as will help in seeking these goals.

SEMINAR: THE HUMANITIES IN AMERICAN EDUCATION
FEBRUARY 16, 1951

Chairman: Harry J. Carman, Professor of History and Dean Emeritus of Columbia College, Columbia University

Participants

Jacques Barzun, Professor of History, Columbia University

Lyman Bryson, Professor of Education, Teachers College, Columbia University

Irwin Edman, Professor of Philosophy, Columbia University

Frank D. Fackenthal, Consultant, Carnegie Corporation

Arnold Graeffe, Associate Professor of Humanities, University of Florida, Gainesville

A. Whitney Griswold, President, Yale University

Barklie McKee Henry, Trustee; Director, United States Trust Company

Charles S. Johnson, President, Fisk University

Robert M. MacIver, Professor of Political Philosophy and Sociology, Columbia University

Millicent McIntosh, President, Barnard College

Reinhold Niebuhr, Professor of Applied Christianity, Union Theological Seminary

Samuel C. Park, Jr., Vice President and Secretary, John Hay Whitney Foundation

Ralph Barton Perry, Professor of Philosophy, Harvard University

Harold Taylor, President, Sarah Lawrence College

Ordway Tead, Chairman, Board of Education, New York City; Editor, Harper & Brothers

Helen C. White, Professor of English, University of Wisconsin

Mrs. John Hay Whitney

John Hay Whitney

The recommendations growing out of this seminar led to the decision that the programs of the Foundation would be in the field of the humanities and to the appointment of a *Humanities Committee* which was to serve as a general advisory committee to the Foundation and also as the nucleus of a selection committee for the John Hay Fellowship Program and for the Whitney Visiting Professors.

The Humanities Committee

Harry J. Carman, Chairman, Dean, Columbia College, Columbia University, 1951–1964

William C. DeVane, Dean, Yale College, Yale University, 1951–1965

Frederic Ernst, Deputy Superintendent of Schools, New York City, 1951–1953

John Hope Franklin, Professor of History, University of Chicago, 1961–1963

Christian Gauss, Dean Emeritus, Princeton University, 1949–1951

Charles S. Johnson, President, Fisk University, 1951–1956

Russell Lynes, Harper's Magazine, 1953–1960

Millicent McIntosh, President, Barnard College, 1951–1952

Thomas C. Mendenhall, President, Smith College, 1953–1965

Marjorie Hope Nicolson, Columbia University, 1952–1954

Charles Odegaard, Dean, College of Literature, Science and the Arts, University of Michigan, 1951–1952

Esther Raushenbush, President Emeritus, Sarah Lawrence College, 1955–1965

Ordway Tead, New York City Board of Education, 1954–1957

Cyril Woolcock, Principal, Hunter College High School, 1951–1964

Administrative Staff 1949–1971

Robert C. Weaver, Director, Opportunity Fellowships, 1949–1956

Charles F. Jones, Program Director, Opportunity Fellowships, 1955–1964

Georgene Lovecky, Coordinating Secretary; Program Secretary, Whitney Visiting Professors and Whitney–Fulbright Visiting Scholars, 1949–1959

Florence E. Dickerson, Administrative Officer, 1952–

Part One

THE OPPORTUNITY FELLOWS

Chapter 1

THE BEGINNINGS
of the
OPPORTUNITY
FELLOWSHIP PROGRAM

The first Opportunity Fellows were appointed in 1950. It was a simpler time than 1970. It was a world in which, however deeply blacks, or Chicanos, or Indians felt that a flourishing American culture was not for them, the dominant Americans were little aware of the sense of deprivation, of how deep it was. By 1970 enough had been said and done to make clear that the problems of individuals and groups who have not had a chance to profit by what this society can provide, educationally, economically, politically, and in all the other ways, are problems of the whole society as well as of individuals and particular groups. We are all involved in unresolved dilemmas together.

The Foundation has an enviable record of dealing with individual problems; the men and women who have had Opportunity Fellowships have an impressive record of dealing with urgent human and social needs in the years following the fellowships, as the story in the following pages indicates.

Many, if not most, of the Opportunity Fellows would have been unable to prepare for professional life without the fellowship. One who later held a Guggenheim Fellowship and a National Science Foundation Fellowship and was invited to spend a year at the Center for Advanced Study in the Behavioral Sciences at Stanford, who is now a distinguished professor of anthropology and is engaged in research and action important in the development of his Indian tribe, says of the Opportunity Fellowship: "It permitted me to secure my Ph.D. and launched me in my professional career. I am extremely grateful for this aid when I was most in need of it."

Another Fellow writes: "My graduate studies cost a great deal beyond the Opportunity Fellowship but the Fellowship put me in a position that made other grants possible." His fellowship started him on the way to a law degree that has made him an important defender of civil rights.

A doctor tells us: "With the Fellowship I was able to start my medical education—'prove' myself—and then I was eligible for university fellowships." This physician is active in dealing with public health problems in a crowded Mexican American community.

Most of the Fellows in academic fields followed conventional courses of academic study, some having been given fellowships as soon as they had finished undergraduate work, others only after the passage of years. A few grants were made to men and women who had no college degree but who had plans for study that the Foundation wanted to support. What some of these plans were will be told later. Obviously the careers of the musicians, painters, and writers who held fellowships took a different course, and their story will be told later, too.

The John Hay Whitney Foundation was established in 1946. The Opportunity Fellowship Program was its first project. It was stimulated by the interest of its first consultant, Edwin M. Embree, and its mission was described in a report by Charles Johnson, president of Fisk University, who served as consultant to the Foundation after Mr. Embree's death:

> The Opportunity Fellowships grew out of an inescapable observation of the uneven distribution of social and cultural opportunity in our economy which, for its most wholesome functioning, assumes a common base line for the free play of individual ability. There are many opportunities available to American youth for securing individual assistance in the form of scholarships, internships and grants-in-aid at critical points in their beginning careers. The assumption is that any youth, with the will and the energy, has an equal chance to win this extra advantage. However, this process of natural selection of talent has not reached deeply enough into the marginal

4

areas of our national life, and thus has passed over human resources of great potential value to our society....

These fellowships were basically an investment in people, but people whose future was not so clearly defined as that of the average American youth, because they were the youth of America's minority populations, only partially in the stream of American culture and life....

The extent to which they have been isolated makes them dependent primarily upon their own leaders for guidance and encouragement and for the incentives that come from individual success in any specialized field. At such a time as the present, when the nation is moving toward the lessening or removal of artificial barriers, the development of notable talent in these groups not only serves the cause of equality of opportunity and national security, but it also accelerates understanding and appreciation for the varied racial and national backgrounds which are American.

The principal recipients of fellowships have been blacks, Mexican Americans, American Indians, and Puerto Ricans, although some awards have gone to men and women in the Pacific Island Trust Territories, and a few to people living in Appalachia. For the first fifteen years Japanese Americans and Chinese Americans were eligible to apply; but Orientals were better able to compete for aid through ordinary channels than the others in whom the Foundation had interested itself. As this became clear the Foundation decided to reserve the funds for those who needed them most. In the early 1950s there were also persons displaced from their homes in Europe during and after the war, and for the first years of the program urgent cases of need among them were also recognized by fellowships.

The number of black applicants has always outrun by a good deal the number of any other group, even allowing for their greater numbers in the population. In the early years it was difficult to get applications from Spanish-speaking men and women, from Indians, and from blacks in the South. This condition has changed to some degree. Among the applications for 1969–70 fellowships there were enough from highly qualified Mexican Americans to cause the Foundation to add $25,000 to its total fund for that year so that more fellowships could be granted to them without depriving other groups. The number of applications from Indian candidates has always been uneven—Indians have not yet become accustomed to expect this kind of aid, and suitable candidates are not as visible as others are. We need better ways than we have had to seek out Indians whose university education should be supported. Each year a few applications come in from the Trust Territories, and the recipients of fellowships have had effective careers in government and other aspects of public life, and in the educational development of their countries. In recent years applications from blacks have been much more widely distributed than they were to begin with. In the earlier years most of them came from urban centers; in the past few years more of them have come from the South and from small communities.

It was only when the people charged with selecting fellowship recipients began to watch the applications come in that some of the intangible personal and psychological factors in the lives of men and women we were seeking became clear. There has always been a lot of casual talk about lack of motivation for higher education among Mexican Americans, or about lack of concern among Indians for the things that would make them a full part of the American society. This kind of talk reproaches them for not doing what presumably anyone would do to improve his lot. But, as I indicated earlier, these minorities are becoming conscious of the hindrances embedded in the society itself that keep them from functioning fully. And the increasing articulateness of both Mexican Americans and Indians about their position in this country has made the rest of us conscious of issues we should have been sensitive to long ago.

Repeatedly the applications of Mexican Americans speak of the pessimism of their people about being able to achieve and keep a place in the community above the simplest level. There is reason for this pessimism. Less than 20 percent, by the last census, of Mexican American males in the five southwestern states were employed at anything other than hand labor. Their wages are low, even where farm mechanization has promoted them above stoop-labor jobs.

The evidence that men and women with Mexican roots have low status in the economy has become painfully clear in the past few years as growing interest in this problem has provided more accurate information, and as more publicity has followed. Studies made by government, by interested social scientists (some of them Mexican American), and by the new political organizations reveal how few Mexican Americans, even where they are a large part of the population, have managerial or professional jobs in industry, or even high-level technical jobs, and how many are production workers or laborers.

The tragic gap in the educational patterns of the Mexican American and the Anglo in the same community is testimony to the failure to assess and meet the needs of the bilingual children in schools in which two languages have been a hurdle rather than an opportunity. Dropout rates are high; whereas the average Anglo child in the Southwest completes twelve years of school, the Mexican American child completes eight. Galarza, Gallegos, and Samora, in *Mexican Americans in the Southwest* (1969), tell us, "As an ethnic group the Mexican Americans have a present handicap of from four to seven years vis-à-vis the rest of the population. The rapid general increase in high school and college enrollment of the recent past serves but to emphasize the gap." And in a town in Arizona, a stable, slowly evolving community with 5,000 inhabitants, mostly Indians and Mexican Americans, only thirty-eight young people graduated from high school between 1910 and 1965 and none completed college.

The story of the attitude of the educationally successful Mexican American toward this problem is told more fully later, but here it is worth reminding ourselves of the circumstances the Opportunity Fellowships were created to change and the reasons for the skepticism among the minority groups themselves about the possibility of change.

In 1971 an intelligent, sophisticated woman who has been actively working on the economic problems of Mexican migrants and whose sympathies are strong, was heard to say impatiently, "Is there any group in this country so *resistant* to education as the Indians?" It is a common comment revealing a common ignorance. The educational situation of the Indians is somewhat different from the situation of the Spanish-speaking people who live in Mexican American communities in the large cities. In attempting to persuade Indians living in reservations to incorporate themselves into the American culture we have shown little awareness, until lately, of the importance of not trying to destroy their ties with their native heritage in the process. Our educational programs for them have been directed toward removing them from their own culture, not building on it, viewing it as a liability not an asset. Our failure to understand and value the varied racial and national backgrounds which are American has led us to think of the education of Indian youth in the same terms as we think of the education of boys and girls who belong to the dominant culture.

The Indians have been unwilling and unable to tear themselves from their roots, and the schools to which they have been sent have created problems for them sometimes even greater than the problems of the Spanish-speaking children of the barrios who come to schools designed for Anglo children. Only now have enough of them transcended the problems to be articulate and persuasive about what must be done to correct for this kind of neglect, which certainly, as much as their native disposition, accounts for their skepticism about education. It is important to note that the most intellectual and sophisticated of the Indians among the Opportunity Fellows have kept their connection with their tribes and work with and for them, however completely they are assimilated into the general culture.

We have lived by a very narrow view of a melting pot—a view that a country made up of people from a wide variety of cultural, religious, and intellectual backgrounds would prosper by reducing that variety to a single culture. In the process we have ignored the values of pluralism and have created a social, political, and economic hierarchy which has elevated the "Anglos" and depressed most those who deviate most from the dominant culture. The American Indians, native to the country, living on reservations, and deeply attached to their past, are perhaps the most dramatic example of this; but all the men and women in this program have been subject to the same kind of discrimination and have suffered the same kind of social, economic, and political deprivation as a result.

We will see later how many of the black Opportunity Fellows—in law, political science, medicine, anthropology, and sociology, and in teaching and public affairs—are participating in educational reforms that take account of the history, the culture, and the concerns of the black people.

Opportunity Fellows, especially those in an area where their group is large, will be an important force in the generation ahead—those now teaching in the universities, those teaching in schools for small children, those training other teachers, school administrators, university professors, social workers and public administrators. These people can help change education to more nearly fit the people to be educated, changing the images and stereotypes that have persisted too long, raising both the possibilities and the expectations of their own people. Without their action this has not been accomplished; with their action it has a better chance of being accomplished.

Chapter 2

THE AMERICAN INDIANS

In 1950–70, the Foundation gave Opportunity Fellowships to eighty-five American Indians. This report gives an idea of who they are, what graduate study they wanted and why, and what they worked at later.

As this was being written, Congress was voting to return to the Pueblo Indians a mountain lake in New Mexico and 48,000 acres of surrounding land, part of a National Forest. The lake has been the spiritual center of tribal life for centuries, and its restitution is a symbol of the fact that most Indians do not want to give up the tribe for simple assimilation into the ways of the American majority, that they are protesting second-class treatment and demanding more of a say in governmental decisions about their lives—loud enough to be heard by many.

Our history is full of events in which, sometimes with good intentions, sometimes not, the non-Indian population has taken action on Indian problems. The General Allotment Act is perhaps the most massive and most obvious of these actions. This law authorized the division of tribal land into individual parcels. On paper this would effect individualization of tribal members, and thus the quicker absorption of the Indians into the mainstream of American life. But no provision, either educational or operational, was made for the Indians themselves to participate in this critical procedure, and a recommendation that the Indian Service become an educational instrument to aid the Indians in developing leadership in handling the new design of life envisaged was never carried out. As more than one writer about the history of those years has pointed out, the assumption was that if funds were appropriated for administering the new law, the very presence of the money would ensure the benefits sought. The people carrying out the program were civil service employees who were under conventional assignments for the use of funds, employment of personnel, and management of property; and too little thought was given to the need to encourage leadership among the Indian people themselves or to train them for the complex and difficult task of administering an entirely new kind of existence.

One positive thing we have learned from our sharper recognition of these problems has been that they cannot be understood or remedied without the active participation of those people who are most urgently involved. In the case of the American Indians, that is, the complicated problems we have lived with since the very beginning of the nation—the Indians' relation to the tribe and their relation to the nation as a whole, their maintenance of an identity as Indians, and their incorporation into American life—are now being confronted more clearly than they have ever been; and with the inescapable knowledge that the accommodations will be made only by the active effort of the Indians themselves working in collaboration with the non-Indian society.

Indians keep their attachment to their tribes, and generalized measures of integrating them into American life—represented mainly by new laws and the administration of these laws by non-Indians—do not suffice.

A highly successful Indian writer, active in university life and at home in any American community, says:

It is the individual and the internal structure of a group to which we must look if we expect to bring about the integration of the Indian people in the general society of the United States. . . . These individuals, if used to build upon, may be the very instruments through whom policy and program can be carried out.

The proportion of Indian applicants for the Opportunity Fellowships has always been much smaller than those from other principal minority groups. The reasons are many. The level of education among Indians is low; the proportion going on to college infinitesimal. Their early schooling on the reservations has by and large been inferior, and their difficulties in keeping up in high school with better-prepared students is very great. Moreover, the problems of adjustment to the world of the college campus are formidable, and until recently little help has been forthcoming to lessen them. The result is that relatively few Indians have gone on to the level of graduate study that is generally expected of an Opportunity Fellow.

Most of the eighty-five Indian Fellows, however fully assimilated into the non-Indian population, have kept important connections with their own and other tribes and have served well in providing the kind of intellectual and practical leadership in a variety of fields that their people most urgently need. Such service ranges from the work of a tribal judge whose activities are primarily inside the structure of his tribe and in communicating and interpreting the life of the tribe to the non-white community, to the distinguished anthropology professor at a major university, all of whose students are non-Indians but whose research and writings deal with his tribe and his part of the country and who serves an important function in the councils of the tribe.

WHO THEY WERE

Indian Opportunity Fellows came from many tribes and many regions of the West and Southwest. As with other Opportunity Fellows, most of them were completing or had completed their undergraduate college education and were ready for graduate study. There were a few interesting exceptions, to be described later.

Most of them had lived a large part of their lives on a reservation. Most had gone to small, little-known state or city colleges, and many were from states in which public education was not particularly distinguished. Most of them began by attending public junior colleges—those we now call community colleges—which usually were within easy reach of their home reservation or actually on the reservation.

Typically it was assumed that the two years of community-college education would be all they would have.

Those who did continue to study moved to nearby state universities; for instance, from Cameron Junior College in Oklahoma to the University of Oklahoma, or from a local community college to South Dakota State University. Some obtained Bachelor of Arts degrees, but a good many took a Bachelor of Science degree, which, in this context, was likely to mean either a teaching certificate or a degree in some quasi-vocational subject, which might lead to technical work of some kind. It is testimony to the increasing hopes for themselves and expectations of themselves that so many students with a limiting educational background, on top of a constricting living situation, were able to accomplish the kind of graduate education that comes so much more easily to young people starting out in the mainstream of American life.

Few of these students attended prestigious colleges as undergraduates, although a number of them later went to the best professional and graduate schools. Two of the women attended well-known private eastern women's colleges as undergraduates.

Several of the applicants who were of mixed white and Indian blood spoke of their mixed race as special hurdles to be overcome. The daughter of an Indian father and white mother says, "The fact that we were part Indian and part white created problems for us in that we were rejected by both groups at first... and for the first 15 years of my life I had no real friends my own age." She lived on the reservation in a one-room shack with her family, her sponsor reported, and it is hard to know whether mixed race or this living environment contributed most to the problems she felt so keenly. It was her exceptional school record, and being chosen by the faculty of her school to attend a citizenship-training program for high school juniors, that helped her classmates begin to look on her as an individual.

Eleven of the eighty-five Indian fellowship holders planned to teach or in some other way be involved in education in elementary or secondary schools. As teachers and administrators all but one of them have been closely identified with their past and their people and have functioned almost entirely within the Indian community, or in its interest. Several of them are now directors or superintendents of Indian agencies under the United States Bureau of Indian Affairs, or are administrators of reservations; these men have also been involved in other government activities relating to Indians. One is on the President's Advisory Committee on Children and Youth, and is also director of Indian Education in South Dakota. Before the fellowship he worked with Indian high school students who wanted to go on to college. Like some other Indian students, he chose for his graduate study the University of North Dakota, as a place that had a special interest in improving educational opportunities for Indians. Mexican American Fellows often choose southwestern universities for parallel reasons.

The applications of the young people interested in the education of Indian children voiced sharp criticism of the procedures followed by the government schools. One of them wrote:

We who deal with Indian children on the plane of community life while attempting to carry out the philosophy of the Indian Service branch of education run up against stone walls. In a democratic state it is assumed that people can, through application of intelligent effort, solve their common problems. We recognize education as a means toward effecting an improved social life. Logically, the objectives of the Indian Service are designed to fit the child to his area. The Birney Day School community is a hodgepodge of about forty log hovels on a barren flat. All but two of them have only one room. Some of them have dirt floors. The bulk of them have two small windows. Although there is an artesian well in the village, most of the families carry water from Tongue River for all their needs. Because of these factors and others, the high morbidity rate is a matter of record. The economy of the village is artificially supported through estate money, lease money, aid to dependent children, old age pensions, relief checks, etc. Our Birney people demonstrate organizational ability in arranging feasts, peyote meetings, give-aways, hand games, dances, and rodeos. These functions appear to be of greater import than consideration of such concerns as health, self-government, administration of schools and the real business of earning a living.

The boys and girls who come to our school represent families of this background.

Helen M. Schierbeck of the Lumbee tribe in North Carolina reported that in her community there were three schools —one for whites, one for blacks and one for Indians. She pointed out: "For many years no studies were attempted above the seventh grade in the Indian schools, and those who finished these seven grades became the teachers in the Indian school."

In 1940 a high school was established, but until 1952 Indians who finished high school could attend only their own college, according to state law. This tribe did not come under federal supervision, and state funds for education were scanty.

Her parents sent her to live with an aunt in Pennsylvania. There she went to school, and then on to Berea College. Her intellectual interests were strong, her concern for international peace passionate, and she obtained an Opportunity Fellowship to take a Master's degree in international relations. Having experienced discrimination as a member of a deprived minority group she hoped she might be effective in working with other deprived people. Mrs. Schierbeck is now director of the Education of American Indians Office, U.S. Office of Education, Department of Health, Education and Welfare.

Like most of the Indian Opportunity Fellows, Alonzo Spang was brought up on a reservation, attended reservation schools, and had a painfully achieved college education. His undergraduate work was taken in two places, with three interruptions for work to support himself. He began as a gravel checker for the Montana State Highway Department, and after a year at college was employed as a clerk by the Bureau of Indian Affairs; he then taught in Indian elementary schools until he obtained his Bachelor's degree, when he began teaching in the high school, where most of his students were Indians. The fellowship gave him a year of uninterrupted study at Arizona State University, where he took a Master's degree in guidance and counseling and went on into the doctoral program in counseling. As he wrote in his application: "The need for guidance and counseling among my people is of the utmost importance. Unless they realize that they must help themselves, they will remain in their present state indefinitely."

The most recent Indian Opportunity Fellowship holders have been able to take advantage of new government aid programs. Juanita Cata is a Navajo Indian who was 34 when she applied for a fellowship. She had taken her undergraduate degree and a Master's degree at the University of New Mexico while she taught in the Albuquerque school system. She learned the importance of dealing directly with the language problems of children from homes where no English was spoken. Two of the schools she taught at, she reported, "had student populations consisting mainly of children for whom English was a second language. Most of the children had racial backgrounds either Spanish American or Negro, and they were also members of the lower socio-economic class."

It was this situation that sent her on to the study of English as a second language, and the fellowship started her on the road to a doctoral degree in that field. She has now finished the Ph.D. course work and is completing her dissertation. She went to Washington in the summer of 1970 as a Civil Service Summer Intern with the White House Conference on Children and Youth and stayed on under an extended appointment through October, preparing a fact book on children to be used at the December conference. She will probably not continue in Indian schools herself but will teach in one of the universities in the Southwest where she can train others in teaching English as a second language.

THE FELLOWSHIPS

ANTHROPOLOGY

Among the most interesting of the Opportunity Fellows, and among those who made the largest intellectual advance and the best use of their time, are the men and women who went into anthropology. Two of the most distinguished among Indian Fellows are in this field; both of them were well on their way before the fellowship year. Alfonso Ortiz, now a professor of anthropology at Princeton University, had a fellowship for his first year of graduate study, and a second one for the final Ph.D. year.

He was born and raised in the Indian village of San Juan, New Mexico. He was the son of a Spanish American mother and an Indian father of the San Juan Pueblo in New Mexico, and had the poverty-ridden childhood of many such children and a more complicated family than most. The effort to live and to go to school was heroic, but scholarships helped him through the University of New Mexico. He wrote:

> I hope to become the finest Pueblo Indian lawyer in the State of New Mexico because I want to help and serve my people, and in attaining a legal education I feel I will fulfill my highest ambition.
>
> I do not pretend to believe that the wrongs done to the Indian people in the past can ever be corrected. I do believe, however, that as assimilation proceeds, there will be many more problems, problems which the Indian people can cope with only through properly trained leaders and through education.

As an undergraduate he had a good liberal arts education which included mainly sociology and anthropology but also philosophy, political science, psychology, literature, and history. These he felt would be important for his life as a person and a lawyer, and he applied to the Foundation for a fellowship to be used at the Georgetown University Law Center in

17

Washington. He was granted one, but before entering law school he wrote about a change in plans:

> After much advisement, consultation, and soul searching, I have decided that the study of law is not for me. Instead I will work towards a Master's degree in Sociology at Arizona State University. [He planned to minor in Indian Education.]
>
> After that I plan to go to the University of Chicago for a Doctorate in Anthropology.

He has the interest of the scholar and the intellectual in his background and his people, as he plans to analyze the social life of the people, and their relations with the people of neighboring Indian and Spanish villages. He was concerned, even in his student years, in defining factors of stability and instability, and suggesting future trends.

At the time of his study he wrote of an interest in teaching anthropology in one of the state universities in the Southwest, and continuing research on the Indian and Spanish-speaking peoples in the Southwest and in Latin America. His long residence in the Southwest and his active participation in local and regional Indian affairs are parts of his experience, knitted into his plans and expectations as a scholar.

One of the men he worked with at Chicago said of him: "I think he has an approach to the present condition of the American Indian in the Southwest that will contribute something really new: he sees the Indians in their present day socio-political context in a way that few others do." In him the intellectual quest was dominant very early, however strong his personal, subjective motives for studying the Indians as a people.

A number of Indians who have studied anthropology under the Opportunity Fellowship Program have found it an important road to travel for self-identification. Robert Vaughan Dumont, a Sioux Indian, grew up on a reservation in Montana, and took his B.A. at Montana State University. He had an undistinguished undergraduate record which his sponsor describes as reflecting a poor schooling situation in childhood and, possibly, a poor college faculty. Dumont's application stated:

> In my work on Pine Ridge [on a research project conducted by Emory University] and my growing up on the Fort Peck Indian Reservation in Montana, I have encountered countless Indian people unable to come to terms with themselves in the world that is created by and for them; and even when their surface personalities profess prosperity and "assimilation," there is a continuous conflict that wages in their mind. This only disappears, I feel, in generations and not in the age of one man. The eradication of this conflict is still to come.
>
> I have attempted to come to terms with what I cited above. I found myself inadequate. In doing this, it seemed that only the present lives had to be understood, in order to define their meaning. I worked with this in creative writing, using personal experiences, anything that I could remember or knew in order to show this. I was unsuccessful and ran into countless obstacles. It seems now, in order to understand what is happening to the people at home and other Indian people like them and to myself, it is necessary to know their past (a pure traditionalism) and what lies in front of them (Western culture). With a knowledge of these two things and an awareness of present transition of these people, I could better understand the meaning of their lives.

In his application for the fellowship he said he expected to go to a small university, out of fear that he could not compete in a large city or a large institution. Since he left the university he has been active in the interest of Indians, although not working as an anthropologist. He was on the steering committee of the American Indian Capital Conference on Poverty; on the board of the United Scholarship Service, and on the Indian Advisory Committee of Upward Bound.

Previously, in the early 1950s, two men and a woman were given Opportunity Fellowships to work in anthropology, who did not complete the work for the Ph.D. All three wanted to study acculturation problems—how the Indian in a strange environment responded to the new world. One studied the adjustment of Indian students entering the University of New Mexico; another, the acculturation and reorientation process in an Indian boarding school.

The anthropological interests in the 1960s were of a different character. Four young Indians were given Opportunity Fellowships to study anthropology in the stirring years between 1964 and 1968. The interest, the approach to the study of the subject, have changed.

One is a Zuñi who lived on a reservation in New Mexico, did her undergraduate work at Stanford, and with the Opportunity Fellowship went to Radcliffe for her M.A. and continued to the Ph.D.:

> My purpose in doing graduate work in Anthropology is to prepare for both teaching and research in the field. However, this purpose must be considered in relation to my particular interest within the field which is cultural change, specifically, the psychological aspects of cultural change. This interest stems directly from my own experience with change, both as it has affected myself and as it has, and is, affecting my tribal community.

This girl's father was a leader in the Indian community in New Mexico, she had been two years in the Peace Corps, and she had taught in a Pueblo day school.

Another applicant wrote: "My long range professional objective is to work in applied Anthropology dealing with American Indians.... I am most interested in finding ways whereby the Indian people themselves will take the initiative in defining their needs and implementing the programs necessary to cope with these needs."

SOCIAL WORK

A large proportion of the Indian Fellows has wanted to go into social work. One wants to work with children because the pressures and strains of the society on minority group children are strong and great adjustment is demanded of them. One, employed as a postal clerk, wanted to study psychiatric social work and join a mental hygiene clinic in the hope of finding ways to alleviate the conflicts within people that usual relations between the races seem to create. This man says he does not expect to gain financially by entering social work—"my modest salary as a postal clerk is above that of the average social worker"—but he feels that such work will make him more comfortable and "increase my self-respect."

Five Indian women in the social work field who held fellowships in the late fifties and sixties give some image of the quality of concern for the needs of their people and the direction this concern gave to their studies. The range is interesting.

One was a woman who had never been to college. She worked as a volunteer with Alcoholics Anonymous in Los Angeles jails, rehabilitation agencies, hospitals. "Hundreds of Indian families are moving here from the reservations each year. The problems they face are terrific," she wrote. (This was in 1954 after the Termination Act.) A social worker with the Rehabilitation Division of the Police Department spoke of her as having "real compassion for people and a lot of insight into the emotional and social problems of American Indians trying to adjust to urban living. She can communicate with them with a readiness that the Indian does not grant a non-Indian." Without a college degree, full professional training in social work was not possible for this woman, but she was able with the fellowship grant to take courses in sociology, anthropology, psychology, group work, and casework counseling. After a year she joined the staff of the Los Angeles Indian Center and worked at welfare problems, counseling, and even fund raising.

Three other women have had very active social work careers rooted in the Indian community but involving them in professional and public service activities. They are important liaison people between the white community and the Indians, while their main professional attention has been on the needs of the Indians themselves. One, a supervisory social worker for the Bureau of Indian Affairs in Oklahoma, handles services for a four-county area of Indians. She deals with financial assistance and housing assistance and educational needs of Indian children, and does casework of all kinds. Her specific interest has been in her own people since her childhood. Another woman is a social worker in a veteran's hospital in Oklahoma, active on the Executive Committee of the Cherokee Nation and on the board of directors of an Indian hospital of the U.S. Public Health Service in Oklahoma. As an avocation, she devotes several hours each week to Cherokee tribal affairs. The third Fellow, now coordinator of Indian Affairs at the University of Minnesota, is on the Mayor's Commission on Human Relations in Minneapolis.

Gloria Emerson, who received a grant in 1969 for a year at Harvard had spent four years before her fellowship working on the Navajo reservation as a social worker, employed by the Office of Navajo Economic Opportunity. She had helped Indians try to work with the white people who have been so fully in control of their fate; but her concerns mark the quality of spirit of many of the young Indians:

> The study of governments is an increasing concern of mine. This concern became actualized this past year when with other Navajos we led a short term movement, questioning the drift of our Navajo Tribal Government. Afterwards two of us interviewed about 60 Navajo people, from over the reservation from all walks of life, about their views of their government. The older Navajo citizens are genuinely concerned but have few constructive ideas which would resolve some of the weaknesses inherent in the tribal government. Younger Navajos are alarmingly apathetic and if not, are critical of the government as belonging to a passing generation of Navajos. It is a rare person who is well-informed about the weaknesses and the strengths of the governing body. These experiences of mine are leading me to one conclusion, that the Bureau of Indian Affairs, parochial and public schools, are doing very little to help resolve some of these profound questions which affect all American Indians. Since the demonstrations against the Tribal

Council, August 1968, I have been immersed in development of two projects and fund-raising activities setting forth some "plugs" to these loopholes. I recognize that these small projects are not comprehensive.

She returned to the reservation after the fellowship year, writing for Navajo adolescents, teaching at Ramah, the first Navajo-controlled high school, and collecting Indian materials for teaching; and is interested in starting community-wide evening high school classes.

Indian social workers have in some cases helped to improve relations between white persons and Indians. A Cherokee who began his study in one of the small rural colleges so many of them start in—this time the College of the Ozarks—went on after the two years there to the University of Chicago for a B.A. It took ten much-interrupted years for him to finish his undergraduate work—he was serving as a field agent for Indian Agency community workers. After his B.A. he was a caseworker for the Oklahoma Department of Public Welfare and then a community worker for the Cherokee Foundation, which is supported by tribal funds. He visited Indian families, participated in community activities involving Cherokees, discussed problems with the chiefs of various bands, and encouraged young Cherokees to seek vocational and academic training.

In applying for the fellowship, he wrote: "These past three years [working directly with the Cherokees through the Foundation] more than any other experience, have made me feel inadequate to serve people in their distress." And he enrolled in classes at the University of Oklahoma.

Many of the applicants for fellowships are of mixed white and Indian blood. The comments of one applicant raise the question whether mixed blood creates special identity problems to cope with, and whether objectively they have advantages over the full-blood Indians:

I have the feeling that our full-blood Cherokees are not taking advantage of local services; that is to say, the less the degree of Indian blood, the more participation in local activities. Also, we have what is described as Indian communities. It seems to me that Indian adults and children who live in these areas are very reserved and inclined to be backward in sociability, education and means of livelihood. At the other extreme, I have found that Full-bloods who live in white dominated communities are as aggressive and uninhibited as their next door neighbor. I should like to know more about these situations. Our people are in a transition period from Indian Department Services to State and County Services. I feel that somehow the Full-blood may be lost in the shuffle unless he is somehow helped along.

He fears for their ability to deal with an increasingly unprotected situation:

The general public is of the opinion too often that the Cherokees have accomplished the ultimate in integration. When we hear or read that a Cherokee is up in the front line of politics, education, law, business, etc., we may generalize and say to ourselves that the Cherokee nation has no problems, that every member is a solid, progressive citizen. Nearly 100 percent of the time this star on the horizon is a mixed blood. History has produced mixed blood notables.... We know the number of Full-bloods is decreasing, but I am concerned with this group, large or small, as to how ready they are for the transition from Federal supervision to state and local levels.... For the one Full-blood who will be unaffected there may be fifty who would fall a victim of greed. They would lose their homes through legal and illegal sales. I am not upholding the Indian Bureau. From their long history of work with the Indian groups it appears that a good job has not been done in helping the Indian to help himself; but the Government presently has the responsibility of protecting their lands from encroachment by others.

Now, ten years after the Master's degree in social work, he continues with the Cherokees as a member of the Cherokee

Executive Committee, and is now working for the Social and Rehabilitation Services of the Oklahoma Department of Institutions.

LAW

The relation of Indians to the law is perhaps more complicated than that of any other minority group in the country. Indians live, as citizens of the country and as members of their tribes, under a dual legal system which creates special problems. In addition, in the past decade, questions of their legal rights have become even more complicated as the Termination Act changed the relations of tribes to the central government, as non-Indian interests have sought more land, and as Indians have been faced with problems of relocation and land sale and with other issues affecting their economic and political lives.

There was a group of Indian applicants in the legal field who had no parallel in other minorities—tribal judges, or tribal court clerks who needed a year free from their duties to visit courts of other tribes and non-Indian courts to improve their service in their own courts, or in some cases to take law studies for particular purposes. These men did not seek a law degree.

One of the tribal judges wrote of his need not to be isolated but to have the opportunity to meet others of his kind: "The differences between Anglos and Indians are not in the areas of needs or desires—in these they are alike—but the ways in which the Papagoes are accustomed to meet their needs are often different from the ways Anglos meet theirs."

A clerk of a tribal court on the San Carlo Indian Reservation needed to find out how comparable officials off the Reservation carry out their duties. He, like others, did not want (and was not eligible for) a degree program in law; he could find the studies and experience he needs outside a degree program.

There have been relatively few requests to the Foundation for support for conventional legal training on the part of Indians. Indeed, the records show only four or five men who have wanted to take law degrees either for general purposes or for the special purposes of their tribes. In the case of a person concerned with public affairs and civil rights, a law degree can lend status and force to his intention to be active in the Indians' behalf. One applicant wrote:

> I have always felt that I could be more effective in Indian affairs with a law degree which would necessitate a specialization in Indian matters such as Indian Land Law or Treaty Rights, but no matter how right or exacting are facts that are uncovered with specialized training they must be interpreted in the language and ways that the Indian and the Whiteman understands which will bridge the gap between the two cultures. It is my sincere feeling that the bridge for this gap is also the foundation of this great country and that is the democratic process. The Indian must be made aware of the mechanics of the democratic process, that if we as American Indians are going to have a better or improved social and economic status, we as individual Indians must take the initiative to better our condition by individual and independent action in contrast to depending on the Federal Government for most of our services in the fields of land management, health, education, and welfare.

A young Cherokee applied for an Opportunity Fellowship to allow him to take his final year at the Harvard Law School. This young man—who had had jobs as laborer, janitor, doorman—had worked in a Southwest Indian Mission, and helped at the Intermountain Indian School. He graduated from Brigham Young University in the top third of his class. A principal part of the third-year program at Harvard is a paper on the student's elected field of study. He reported:

> I intend to write a paper analyzing the legal history of the American Indians in their relationship with the Federal Government and the present significance of that history.
> I will use the degree in practice on an Indian reservation or will enter the Federal Management Intern pro-

gram in the Bureau of Indian Affairs. In any case I intend to associate myself with the Indian "cause" and hope to help in the formation of administrative policy in regard to Indians. Since my wife is Navajo, I am especially interested in the highly developed legal department which that tribe has. My own tribe has no legal department as such.

A small number of Indian Opportunity Fellows have been interested in law apart from Indians' legal concerns. Like some of the people in the social sciences, a few of them have been interested in international cultures—one or two have wanted to study law in order to go into the diplomatic corps.

Another applicant makes no mention of concern with Indian problems; he had a plan of work that reflects a dominant current concern of young people across the country:

> I am interested in the relationship of law to urban society. The problems associated with the rapid development of cities have produced a need for lawyers with knowledge of urban legal questions. A number of law schools have responded to this need by adding courses which deal with the problems of metropolitan areas. The topics vary from land use planning and local government law to important aspects of family law and of the legal protection of civil rights. My main interest lies in the last two areas.
>
> One of the most tragic products of urbanization has been what often appears to be a chronic culture of poverty. The major crises of this century will probably occur in the blighted ghetto areas of the city, whose citizens are frequently victims of economic and social inequalities which a just legal system is supposed to prevent. Admittedly, however, poverty knows no boundary between the urban and rural, and through study of urban legal problems one can often discover solutions which are also applicable in rural areas. One example of program, the concept of which is appropriate to both urban and rural areas, is the Office of Economic Oppor-

tunity's establishment of neighborhood law offices. The legal sector of OEO is employing an increasing number of lawyers in neighborhood law offices to represent the poor, to aid citizen groups in opposing injustices and in striving to better their communities.

I have chosen this course of study because it is relevant to society and society's problems. The United States is fully capable of providing economic and social justice for all its citizens. Urban law is one of the tools which can be employed to this end, and I want to be able to use this tool effectively.

This recent applicant had a B.A. from the University of Redlands in California and an M.A. from Harvard in history. He was given a fellowship to begin the study of law at Harvard.

MEDICINE

The medical fellowship holders show a 100 percent record of completion of their studies. This is probably because they had already made a strong commitment when they applied, having been accepted by a medical school and, in most cases having had a year or more of medical studies. They had found ways of helping finance their education. They show all the problems of other Indians, and the picture of the young man with illiterate or lower-working-class parents is common, but some came from a more favored environment—that is from "leadership" families who were able to do more for them than most. There is a strong sense of social consciousness among them. One wrote:

The extreme Eastern section of Oklahoma has principally an agricultural economy. The people living in this region are not as fortunate financially as the people living in the wheat or oil districts of the State. For this reason, and also because of the scarcity of modern hospitals, not many young doctors are willing to start practice there. This region of Oklahoma is my home. I know the people, their problems and outlook on life and I want to continue, after graduation to live among them.... I cannot recall my considering anything else except becoming a good country doctor.

Another wrote: "Eventually I plan to open a general practice in a small town of 5000 or so. I will be able to give medical attention to families who do not trust white people."

And another: "The work that needs to be done in medicine and the people that need medical care is no less a stimulus than my desire to be myself and set some sort of example for others of my race."

The last of these, five years after the award, married to a nurse, was described as a country doctor serving a huge area. Five years after that he won the Indian Achievement Award of the Indian Council Fire, and in 1967 the American Cancer Society Award. He was then a practicing physician in Woodlake, California, and on the staff of several hospitals.

Fellows have gone into various aspects of public health, and a number of them work in health centers in Indian areas. One is a deputy director of a health center sponsored by the Division of Indian Health; another is a public health doctor on an Indian reservation; others are physicians in veterans' hospitals in Arizona and California, where there are Indian patients. One is chief of staff in a hospital in Oklahoma and director of his County Health Department.

One of these medical Fellows has a wider and more cosmopolitan career than most of the others. His expectations were quite modest; the application stated:

The ultimate end I wish to reach is to become a doctor and practice among my fellow tribesmen. The community in which I live is twenty miles from the nearest doctor and is in definite need of a physician. Furthermore, there has never been a Kiowa Indian who has become a member of the medical profession. I feel that the Kiowas are in need of leaders and certainly in the next several critical years will need leaders more than ever. A doctor would be in a key position to help them in several ways.

He has, however, lived less within tribal confines than most of the others. He won a series of fellowships after receiving his degree—from the National Foundation of Infantile Paralysis and from the National Institutes of Health. He was elected to membership in the honorary medical fraternity. He had a long army career and reached the rank of major. He was consultant to the University of Oklahoma and then became a member of the faculty of medicine and microbiology at the university's School of Medicine.

One of the most distinguished of the Indian Fellows dealing with health problems was not a physician but a speech pathologist. She was one of very few Indians to attend as an undergraduate any college outside of a state system. Evelyn Yellow Robe Finkbeiner, a Sioux Indian from Rapid City, South Dakota, went to Mount Holyoke College, from which she was graduated magna cum laude. She taught speech at Vassar for six years, took a Master's degree and applied for an Opportunity Fellowship to complete at Northwestern her work for a Ph.D. in speech correction. She completed this in 1954 and was awarded a Fulbright Fellowship to study and continue research on cancer of the larynx. A year later she had an appointment as lecturer in the Medical School of Northwestern University, where she taught until 1959. She married a doctor, head of obstetrics at a hospital in Germany where she has since lived. She has been doing research, writing, editing, and lecturing abroad and occasionally in this country.

OTHER PROFESSIONS AND BUSINESS

Men who received fellowships to work in architecture, political science, public administration and business have used their training in the interest of their own tribes or of the Indian population generally. An Alaskan Indian, then a credit officer in the Alaska Native Service, asked for funds to study banking methods, cooperatives, and credit systems so that he might further the existing cooperative program in Alaska.

He left school early to support his mother and sisters; five years later he came back, worked his way through high school, attended a normal school briefly, and then had no more formal education. He became interested in politics and was elected mayor of his town, and for five years was Territorial Grand President of the Alaska Native Brotherhood. He worked with unions; he worked to get legislation which finally made it possible for Indians and Eskimos to serve in the territorial legislature. In his fellowship application he wrote of that time:

> Needless to say, more high salaried positions have been offered to me than any other man in the Territory. I have always turned the offers down because of political complications that were sure to follow. Pressure became so great that I fled to a Federal position in the Native Service in order to do the type of work I liked and knew best without hindrance.

Support made it possible for this man to leave his job and get the training he needed. The first part of his fellowship year (1952–53) was spent as an apprentice in a Denver bank and attending courses in accounting. The second semester he attended business courses at the university and won a United Nations Fellowship for study of cooperatives in Nova Scotia. He returned to Alaska and worked with Indians on their boat and cannery loans, and two years later was the credit officer of the Bureau of Indian Affairs. From 1962 on he was a member of the Human Rights Commission for the State of Alaska.

Andrew Acoya, now on the faculty of the University of New Mexico, studied architecture at the Massachusetts Institute of Technology. He had worked as a laborer, then as a truck driver, finally as a draftsman with the Bureau of Indian Affairs, had worked with the Model Cities and Urban Renewal Program for low-income housing in Albuquerque, and had written a Bachelor's thesis at the University of New Mexico on Pueblo housing. From the beginning, his interest in architecture was in low-income housing, particularly for American Indians. At MIT he studied in the program for housing and community design for low-income families and is involved with studies and designs for the housing of South American Indians who have become squatters in large urban centers. His teachers were an architect from Argentina who has lived and worked in South American cities and an architect-sociologist who has worked in the barrios of South America. He wants to advance the chance of Southwest Indians –

> [to] develop their lives in an environment best suited to their very special and unusual situations. Their surroundings (totally) I feel are extremely important at the present time when a chaotic world envelops them and seeks to enter a part of their own small but stable domains. The social and economic changes which they make (if they wish to do so) will evolve a great deal from an environment which may aid or hinder them—this is my major concern, the development of surroundings which will be beneficial to the Indian people.

He has been on the faculty of the University of New Mexico and has been using that university's facilities to give Pueblo Indians advice on matters of housing and planning. He has made plans for economically feasible development projects that can be funded through public or private agencies —a good illustration of a man working at the grass roots level and using the widened knowledge he has been able to get by working with men interested in the same problems in other contexts.

In 1951 the Foundation awarded a fellowship to the superintendent of the Ford Berthold Indian Reservation, who held Bachelor's and Master's degrees from South Dakota State University, to complete a Ph.D. in public administration at Harvard. He was considerably older than most applicants and had had nearly twenty years of experience in the federal service—as an adviser in an Indian school, a farm agent for the Indian Bureau and a tribal relations officer, before becoming superintendent of his reservation.

His need for the kind of study the fellowship would afford was urgent. As a result of the decision to construct the Garrison Dam, a thousand people living on the reservation had to be relocated. He assisted in determining what money settlement should be made for the lands the reservoir plan required, and in developing a program for relocation of the displaced tribe:

> This relocation, when accomplished, will involve a complete reorganization of the government services as to facilities and functions. It will also call for a re-establishment and re-orientation of the community and economic life of the 20,000 people that live on the Reservation. The assignment calls for the use of all the help obtainable and available in the research applicable from the natural and social sciences. One way to do this was to go directly to one of our leading universities in search of such aid.

With the help of Harvard University he entered the School of Public Health, and with the aid of the Foundation he was able to continue for his Ph.D. degree.

Like most Indians in public service programs he not only was concerned to provide assistance for this particular project but also felt that "it can have practical meaning for other tribes of Indians that are imminently facing similar relocation problems in the coming development of the Missouri River Basin." During the summers he returned to the reservation to help with the practical work involved in plans for relocation. His project is one that should be a precedent for other fellowship applicants. Of his program Dr. John Gaus of Harvard wrote:

> I cannot imagine a more manageable and appropriate program of research than this one since it constitutes a kind of general staff research for an operating official who will be responsible for carrying out a very complicated program and yet at the same time is a study that has important implications for many other points of adjustment between the physical environment and two or more cultural groups in this and other countries.

Chapter 3

THE MEXICAN AMERICANS*

In the past five years, men and women in the southwestern states bearing Spanish surnames have become increasingly visible to the rest of American society, both as they compel attention to the need for basic changes in attitudes and in action by the dominant society, and as they act to bring changes about. The changes in education, economic condition, and political place that must not only be accepted but also accelerated, could alter the face of large areas of American life, and of "Anglo" conceptions of the Mexican Americans as an integral part of American society.

Mexican Americans have reminded us that they are the second largest minority group in the United States. We are at a place in our history where it is of critical importance that the concept of minority groups with all its connotations must disappear, although it is the very insistence of the society at large on that concept which has finally made the people whom the words designate summon their own strength to act in their own interest.

Nearly a hundred young men and women of Mexican American origin have held Opportunity Fellowships. All of them have experienced the hazards and hurdles faced by all Mexican Americans, who have never been given the oppor-

* This chapter and the following one review the story of Opportunity Fellows with Spanish surnames. Enough of these were men and women who came, or whose parents came, from Puerto Rico, and settled principally in and around New York, to write of them separately (Chapter 4). The Opportunity Fellows discussed in this chapter came principally from the Southwest and all of them have been considered under the heading of Mexican Americans.

tunity to function in the society with an even chance for fulfillment.

Opportunity Fellows give concrete testimony to the problems, the sense of need, and the possibilities of this section
of the American public. The Opportunity Fellows are, as a
group, neither the most submissive nor the most militant
among the Mexican Americans, who have for many years
been unduly silent about their deprivations, their needs, and
their resentments; but now, in the growing conviction that
the deprived must become a full part of American society,
they have ceased being silent.

Many current efforts to change the lot of the poor and the
powerless are directed to those who have been able to achieve
least—who are imprisoned in a ghetto culture. The Opportunity Fellowships were directed toward men and women
who had already demonstrated both talent and achievement
in moving to a more desirable kind of life. The fellowships
sought to increase that possibility. In spite of a disheartening
persistence of racism in the country, these hundred Mexican
American Fellows are providing a kind of leadership that
must be continually enlarged and that will do its part in
changing the lives of others.

WHO THEY WERE

Like other Opportunity Fellows, most of these men and
women had completed college, and some of them were part
way through their graduate or professional study when the
fellowship came along. They form part of the tragically few
Mexican Americans who have reached and completed college.
Over 2,500 students graduated from California colleges in
1964; although people with Spanish surnames are 10 percent
of the California population, less than 1 percent of college
graduates that year had Spanish surnames. In 1967, 12.9
percent of the population of Los Angeles County had Spanish
surnames; 3.3 percent of the Los Angeles graduate students
that year were Mexican Americans.

In the past few years a concerted effort has been made to
remedy this situation. Between 1967 and 1969, a period in
which the total number of graduate students doubled at Uni-

versity of California at Los Angeles, the number of Mexican American graduate students there increased from 54 to 310. So there is some evidence that the great discrepancy is at least being worked at.

A rush of recent literature tells us that there is increasing interest in the universities in the intellectuals of the minority groups who have been neglected, thwarted, and powerless for most of our history and who must take leadership in the coming years. The colleges and universities have belatedly begun to face the consequences of a policy of indifference to the potential of this large section of our society. The need and the possibility for leadership in the educational, intellectual, and professional life of the country has finally begun to be recognized; important in this recognition is a small group of Mexican American teachers and college professors who have maintained an active interest in and connection with their communities. They are giving impetus to the kind of change that will stimulate leadership in others.

The men and women who are being educated for leadership will have to use their leadership to deal with the problems besetting their people—educational, economic, political, legal, and health problems. The Anglo child in New Mexico completes twelve years of school; the Mexican American child drops out by the seventh year. The language problems of a vast number of children who speak only Spanish at home and are compelled to speak only English at school, when they have had no usable training in English, have relegated hundreds of them to classes for retarded children, though they are not retarded except in practice of the English language. Not only education, but health care, economic and political opportunity, and better protection under the law must have the stimulus of leadership from the Mexican Americans themselves.

Increasing awareness of this in the case of blacks in the past few years has not only made their participation in change a national issue, but this begins to take on urgency for other minorities as well. Ten years ago—even five—it was a matter of common concern among those who saw the need for leadership that, as Mexican Americans moved into professional careers and were themselves upward bound, their wish seemed to be to move so fully into the dominant American society as to feel no commitment to their ethnic group. In recent years this has been changing and the change can be noticed in the goals of the men and women in the Opportunity Fellowship program.

In every aspect of the lives of the Mexican Americans, from opportunities for graduate and professional training and the practice of the professions, through political opportunities, through the education of children and adolescents, to their entrance into the labor force, Mexican American leaders must be the agents of change. If less than 20 percent of the Mexican American men in the five southwestern states were during the 1960s employed in non-manual occupations, it will take at least legal, political, and educational changes to remedy the situation. And the Mexican Americans themselves will be central factors in finding the remedies. An interesting development in the Opportunity Fellowship Program, with the increasing awareness of the Mexican American people themselves, has been the changes in intention, even in their choice of places to study, that have come with the change in the general climate over the past few years.

Since 1967, when President Johnson created an Inter-Agency Committee on Mexican affairs, and Mexican Americans themselves have been increasingly vocal, there has been growing attention to these problems by government and by private agencies; the Department of Health, Education and Welfare has been underwriting vocational rehabilitation programs; the Ford Foundation has been financing investigations of Mexican American problems in the five southwestern states. Without trained leadership among the people themselves these efforts will accomplish little, and any new plan for trained leadership will need the counsel and support of the Mexican Americans themselves, or it too will accomplish little.

Most graduate-study fellowships go to people who were given A's and B's in college courses. The Opportunity Fellows selection committee with Mexican American applicants, as with others, has had to look beneath the surface of these academic conventions to find hidden promise; and it has awarded fellowships to some applicants whose credentials were quite unorthodox.

A very high proportion of the Mexican American Fellows completed the work for the degree—whether an M.A., a Ph.D., or a law or medical degree—which the fellowship helped to support. The record of completion is remarkable, considering the number of cases of extreme poverty in the background of these men and women. Again and again there are accounts of houses with no electric lights, towns where a telephone was a luxury, fathers who were manual laborers, some working only intermittently. A large proportion of the applicants not only held jobs throughout their high school and college years but also held full-time jobs—working nights on top of full academic schedules in many cases. Often the Opportunity Fellowship was the first substantial help they received, and it, too, was only partial; indeed, as one reads the records, one sees that their requests for funds were based on the assumption that only minimal help was possible.

Preparation in elementary school has been poor for Mexican Americans in the crowded barrios of the cities and just as bad in rural areas. Describing her part of rural New Mexico, Esther Gallegos y Chavez writes:

> Since the main occupation has been farming, the region has acquired and retained a very pastoral setting and the development of the region has been rather slow. Geographically it is situated in a rather remote area where methods of communication are very primitive and not until fairly recently have buses traversed the terrain. Telephones are still an unheard-of luxury; newspapers are scarce and the few that exist are very provincial in content and expression. The only real means for communication with the outside world affairs is the radio ... and this is very recent....
>
> Education in this part of New Mexico has been even later in coming than it has in the rest of the state. Health education and sanitation have but recently made their debut.... There still remain many villages in Rio Arriba County and in many other parts of the state where the

geographical location has made it impossible to establish schools and have good systems of education. Buildings are one room structures, poorly heated and lighted where few teachers are interested and attracted. Those teachers who do come are often untrained and go there because of their inability to secure positions elsewhere. Recently a new problem has risen. The Catholic Church for many years provided nuns to teach in these isolated areas. There was an arrangement with the State Department of Education whereby they were paid a salary by the state, etc.; however, the state recently has ruled that members of such religious communities may not teach in state owned schools. As a result an even greater shortage of teachers was the outcome.

Her application speaks her intention to become a rural teacher herself and to work for better rural schools.

Many applicants have had broken school careers and present mediocre academic records. The application of Raoul Mora reminds us that when one has to work to support oneself one is unlikely to win academic laurels. Adopted at the age of three, he was left an orphan through the death of both adoptive parents by the time he was four, and went to live with a stepsister:

I was in the 5th grade but I was three years too old for that grade. When I passed to the 6th grade, I went to Mission Junior High School where the majority of the students were Anglo-Americans who had a better grasp of the curriculum and who were better dressed. Since I could not keep up with the Anglo-American students and I was ashamed of my overall appearance, I dropped out of school and ran away from home. I ran out of money in Hereford, Texas, and got a temporary job as a dishwasher in a restaurant owned by Mr. Dudley Green. When September of 1954 came around, he encouraged me to go back to school. I went back and worked my way from the 7th grade through the 12th grade.

I worked for Mr. Green from 2 P.M. to 10 P.M. daily

through the 7th grade when he sold his restaurant. After he sold his business, he got me a job as janitor for Witherspoon Law Firm. I worked from 6 P.M. to 10 P.M. for Mr. Witherspoon five days a week. At the same time I kept books and wrote letters for "Bruna Dept. Store" in return for a place in which to live in the rear of the store. For my meals, I worked from 5 A.M. to 7 A.M. for the "M&M Cafe" as a dishwasher. In 1958, I stopped working for the department store and the restaurant and started working for C.R. Anthony Clothing Store. My income was now coming from the clothing store and the law firm. In May of 1960, I graduated from Hereford High School and joined the U.S. Army.

I was released from active duty in July of 1963 and enrolled at West Texas State University. I married when I was a sophomore, August 14, 1964. I worked most of my way through West Texas State University and whatever additional money I needed, I borrowed from the institution. I graduated May 22, 1967, and enrolled in the School of Law at Texas Southern University September 16, 1967.

He now works for a legal foundation, mainly on consumer problems, tenant–landlord problems, and domestic problems —all areas of importance to the Mexican American community.

In the early years of the Opportunity Fellowships, the typical aim of applicants was to move into the current of American life. But gradually, applicants began to stress their desire to work with and for the people and places where their roots lay. They sought the creation of a mainstream that maintained the identity of all peoples.

The application of a woman law student, Velma Kamalina Montoya, spoke of the help she would be able to bring to the barrios. One factor that influenced her was an experience when she was a junior at Occidental College:

Last spring I was a bilingual interviewer for the study of the urban experiences of students of Mexican extraction in Los Angeles high schools conducted under the auspices of the Rosenberg Foundation. This study and the visits to the diverse Mexican homes which it entailed enabled me to evaluate the needs of the Spanish-speaking community in Los Angeles and to focus my vocational objective.

I plan to obtain a law degree in order that I may act as a bilingual representative for the over one-half million Spanish-speaking people in the Los Angeles area. At present there are only fourteen Spanish-speaking lawyers serving Los Angeles. In my study and later practice of law I plan to concentrate on the legal aspects of a field which has received a minimum of legal emphasis in our community, the field of immigration. Although six thousand Mexican immigrants enter the Los Angeles area every year, today there are only four bilingual lawyers in Los Angeles who specialize in counseling these immigrants as well as the one hundred thousand Spanish-speaking aliens already residing in the Los Angeles area. Today there is not one Mexican American woman serving this community as a legal consultant.

I feel I can perform a worthwhile service by working with Spanish-speaking Mexican and Mexican American women whose culture has not conditioned them to share their problems with men.

The Foundation granted an Opportunity Fellowship to a Mexican American woman who had had no opportunity to go to college at all. For many years Grace Olivarez worked for equality of opportunity for Mexican Americans. She knew that a law degree would help her in this work; with the support of people who knew her work and had confidence in her talents, she applied to the Law School of Notre Dame University, and was accepted, college or no college. Her plans for the future began with what she would do in the two summer vacations of law school:

I plan to work in a legally-related job, and have already solicited employment from various federal agencies, namely, the Office of Economic Opportunity (Legal Services Department); U.S. Civil Rights Commission and Equal Employment Opportunity Commission. It is my plan to do this type of work during the two summer vacations and to learn as much as possible about law and its relation to the impoverished and minority groups.

Mexican Americans have only recently begun to receive attention to their legal problems. Even so, there are very few Spanish-speaking lawyers, Negro or Indian lawyers in the Southwest, and even fewer who have any knowledge of the unique and special needs of the poor among these three minority groups. In addition, there seems to be a reluctance on the part of minority group attorneys to identify with the deprived for fear this identification might retard their assimilation. As a result of surveys and extensive travel I have done in the Southwest, I find a distinct shortage of sympathetic attorneys of any ethnic or racial background, consequently, the impoverished minority groups lack guidance and advice regarding their rights.

It is my feeling that in order to be effective in the Southwest, one has to know and understand this part of America, its geographic, political, informational, ethnic, demographic, economic and religious factors plus its international position. The area lacks social maturity. The lack of long time wealth in the Southwest is obvious in the newer communities. Lack of social identification has led to a scrambling, clawing society. Philanthropy, sparse at best, is confined to "safe" fields such as culture, medicine, music and University chairs. Social progressivism is a virtual stranger. Universities reflect the provincial views of their trustees and principal donors (often the same) in their attitudes toward social mobility. Social statistics are uncommon. Censorship of student studies is not known. New views, new ideas, while entertained, are suspect by virtue of their newness in the community. Thus, the area seems to have more than its share of problems on the scene at present, and the prediction is that the regional population will double in the next fifteen years.

Ethnically, the area has a unique history. Once settled by Indian tribes who migrated further and further south prior to the arrival of gold-seeking Spanish battalions, the area is now populated principally by those of Mexican heritage, those of Spanish lineage, those Negroes who have migrated west, Indians who have retreated to and from reservations, and "Anglos"—those from a European background. Of the 29,000,000 total population, four million persons in the area have Spanish surnames. There are more than 2.2 million Negroes. 189,000 Indians inhabit the area—both on and off the reservation. The balance comes from customary sources.

I plan to practice in Arizona and specialize in law for the poor. Although my knowledge of the Spanish language will be of extreme importance in serving the Mexican American, it is my desire to work also among Indians off the reservations and among Negroes, particularly those in the rural areas of central Arizona.

Ultimately, in addition to the practice of law, I would hope to use my position and economic independence to help bring about much needed cooperation among the above-named culturally different groups and the Anglo American, by serving as a catalyst, a role that is difficult to carry out when one is dependent on the so-called power structure for employment and income.

Why do Mexican American boys and girls drop out of school? As one reason, a social-worker applicant suggests that they feel "there is no reason for pursuing educational goals beyond a certain point, for in the last analysis the color of your skin will determine where your career will terminate."

Applicants for Opportunity Fellowships who want to help the group of which they are a part speak fairly often of the fact that boys and girls need "role models" if they are not to succumb to discouragement. This idea is mentioned especially often by Mexican American applicants; perhaps they consider the need for a role model especially great because of the close ties within the family and within the immediate community. The idea shows up not only in the applications of persons interested in community service but also in those of people

43

interested in scholarly careers for themselves. One of these was Albert Roy Baca, a student of the classics:

I have been encouraged to go ahead by many individuals who have not had the fortune of being second-generation themselves and so were gravely handicapped by the language barrier from fully integrating themselves in the society. They have placed their trust in me. The attainment of my goal shall mean to the community that I have risen above this obstacle. But more important is what my achievement shall mean to those yet younger than myself. I have heard them say: "Why go ahead, what's the good of it?" These are not questions asked with the assurance of logic; they arise and are prompted by a feeling of despair and hopelessness. Many, having never seen one of their own people attain a position of honor and respect in the higher professions, feel that they are doomed to subservience and to an inferior class for the rest of their lives.... As a teacher in the community I shall inspire my pupils to fight and work for the best things our society can offer: dignity and self-respect through achievement.

Part of the usefulness of a role model is that the boy or girl is helped to overcome the sense of inferiority at being a Mexican American in a society dominated by Anglos. The study of Spanish, of its literary style and linguistics, was independently important for a good many of the men and women who sought to carry their education further, but it also became to them an important instrument for the emancipation of others. "When I finish my work," wrote one of them, "I intend to return to the Southwest to teach in one of the colleges or universities, and through the medium of language and literature attempt to promote a program that may lessen the friction caused by the contact of two cultures." Later, when the time came to return with his Ph.D. completed, he wrote: "We are very glad to be able to return to New Mexico, where we may be able to influence young people of Mexican descent to continue their education, and to guide in community affairs as well as educationally." In the ten years after his Opportunity Fellowship, this man was with the Peace Corps in Brazil, served on committees for Office of Economic Opportunity programs, and then made his career as a professor of Spanish and Portuguese in a southwestern university.

The awards committee was interested in encouraging a wide range of talent, and the varied interests of the applicants led to great diversity in the field of training of Opportunity Fellows. Among Mexican Americans there were relatively few applications in the arts and about 10 percent in medicine. There were a good many in law and the social sciences. Many of the Fellows are now teaching on all levels from kindergarten to the universities.

The diversity is suggested by the following notes on the present occupations of (A) the first twenty persons on an alphabetical list of Mexican American Opportunity Fellows and (B) every fifth name from among the rest on the list:

A: 1. Member of faculty of the Stanford University Medical School
   2. Director of a training and research project in Colombia
   3. Assistant dean and professor of education at a state university
   4. Assistant professor of government at a state university and director of a cultural center of the U.S. Information Service in South America
   5. Professor of Spanish in a state university
   6. Teacher in an elementary school
   7. Assistant district attorney
   8. Graduate student in a school of education
   9. Associate justice of a court of appeals
   10. Student of Mexican American history
   11. Medical student
   12. Anthropologist, collecting oral history of Indians
   13. Member of a juvenile parole board

14. Studying music; recipient of an award from the National Institute of Arts and Sciences after the Opportunity Fellowship award
15. Supervisor of child welfare in city schools
16. Art teacher in public schools
17. Professor of sociology in a state university
18. Teacher of English as a foreign language in a university
19. Teacher of history and literature in a university
20. Teacher of classical languages in a state university

B: 1. Superintendent of schools
2. Dentist
3. Associate professor of history in a university
4. Professor of history in an urban university
5. Professor of history in a state university
6. Assistant professor of economics
7. Student at law school
8. Coordinator of leadership and education program for a southwestern city
9. Executive director of a state economic-opportunity organization
10. Consultant to United States A.I.D. program in South America
11. Research on problems in twentieth-century New Mexico history
12. Assistant professor in a state college
13. Writer
14. Teacher of foreign language teachers at a state university
15. Physician

THE FELLOWSHIPS

TEACHERS, SCHOLARS, AND SCHOLAR ACTIVISTS

Some applicants who aimed to be college or university teachers were scholars primarily interested in their own academic discipline. Others however were principally concerned with improving the public schools. And many applicants who planned to be high school or elementary school teachers hoped by their own teaching to change the school experience of Mexican American youngsters. Finally there was a group of prospective teachers and others who might be called scholar activists, since active participation in community affairs was for them an immediate goal. Their graduate work was in political science or history.

A review of the subsequent history of the Mexican American Fellows tells us that many are today involved in efforts to change the really handicapping character of the lower schools, which have consistently ignored the special needs of children for whom English is, in fact, a second language.

Gloria Burchard, a teacher of Spanish and history in a San Francisco school district has written a curriculum for a high school, designed to suit the needs of children whose first language is Spanish; part of it calls for the teaching of some courses in Spanish in a school in which it had never been taught before. Even teaching the Spanish language has been objectionable to many people in the school systems of the heavily Mexican American states. But taking a course in Spanish grammar and composition can, for children whose native language is Spanish, be a significant step both in improving their knowledge of the language and in giving them the dignity that the responsible use of two languages should give any student. A dozen Mexican Americans have used their Opportunity Fellowships to prepare to do the kind of language teaching that they never had as students.

Daniel Castillo straddles the fields of education and law. He recruits students for eastern schools and deals with the problem of segregation in the schools of his town of Corpus Christi, Texas. These schools were found to be de facto segregated with respect to Mexican Americans, in a case in which an Opportunity Fellow, James De Anda, was the lawyer for the plaintiff. As a student, Mr. De Anda served on the Harvard Civil Rights–Civil Liberties Research Committee and as staff assistant in the Community Legal Assistance Office. The law firm in which he serves planned to open a branch office in the economically disadvantaged section of town, probably during 1971. Cases would be taken for a nominal fee or no fee, depending on the client's ability to pay.

Dr. George J. Garza, an early Opportunity Fellow, is superintendent of an independent school district in Corpus Christi and an active participant in job-opportunity activities, committees for community services, vocational education training projects, and other community-oriented services. Dr. Garza applied for an Opportunity Fellowship after having taken a Master's degree in a Texas teachers college and taught for fourteen years in Texas. He was the first American of Mexican origin to graduate from the high school in his town, and the first native son of that town with a Spanish name to graduate from college. He is a force for the development of the capacities of the Mexican American people of his controversial part of Texas.

Julian Samora was an able graduate student well on his way to his Ph.D. when he applied to the Foundation—one of the young men whose talents had already brought him undergraduate and graduate fellowships. The Opportunity Fellowship was to provide him with funds for the final stage of his work. At home himself in both the English- and Spanish-speaking cultures of the Southwest, his concerns for working with the Spanish-speaking people were deeply rooted. He has had an increasingly distinguished career since he completed his studies, both in academic life—he is chairman of the Department of Anthropology and Sociology at Notre Dame —and as a writer and scholar, continuing to call the attention of both professional and lay readers to the needs of Mexican Americans. He directs graduate students in studies in this field; writes on the problems of immigration from Mexico (his latest book is *The Wetback Story*); and he serves widely on commissions and as consultant to foundations, to the government, and to public interest groups concerned with the lives and possibilities of the people in whose interests he has constantly worked.

One of the most distinguished of the educators among the Opportunity Fellows is Julian Nava, who was committed to political action from the beginning. Julian Nava began his college studies in a junior college in East Los Angeles, where his interest in encouraging Mexican Americans to become active in civic affairs started early. He went on to Pomona, and then to Harvard where he completed his graduate studies in History. His interest in political affairs continued throughout his studies and the development of his plans to become a teacher in the Mexican American community. Like Dr. Samora he has had a steadily increasing influence in the affairs of Mexican Americans. He became President of the Board of Education in Los Angeles where this interest was placed in the context of the whole problem of education in that city. It was a time in which Mexican Americans were beginning to speak in a louder voice to call attention to their educational and political needs which had been, here as elsewhere, tragically neglected. He has written and spoken widely, and has now returned to college teaching.

Others for whom community participation was an immediate goal have reported the experiences that made them what we call scholar activists. One man had intended to enter the priesthood, worked in a small village, and became involved in the community council. It was these experiences that impressed him with the need to study further, and he entered graduate school with his Opportunity Fellowship. "When a man like Maldonado comes along he should be encouraged to rectify history," wrote one of his sponsors.

Another man, intending at first only to go on for a Master's degree, spoke of his "cultural marginality" and went on to say: "The single most important factor in my life has been my ethnicity—and the consequence has been an incessant identity crisis." He was born in Texas and spoke no English until he was eight. He went on to take a Ph.D. and wrote then of the debilitating effect on a minority of the present "socializing" process, where two distinct cultures exist.

A Fellow taking a Ph.D. in Mexican studies points out that at four and a half years of age he was picking walnuts, at six working all day in the fields. His father was an unskilled laborer, he himself a janitor and dishwasher. A turn in the Peace Corps helped him to understand Latin American culture and set him on the road to the study of politics and history.

A cultural anthropologist speaks of the "need for well-trained professionals of Mexican ancestry to articulate the problems facing American-born Mexicans, immigrant Mexicans, and migrant Mexicans." This man learned only after he came out of the army that in high school he had been in a program for students who were not college bound; in fact, no one had mentioned college to him.

LAW

Early in this chapter two women lawyers were quoted on the need of the Mexican American community for lawyers who had an understanding of the particular needs of Mexican Americans. Other applicants have testified to the same effect:

The Mexican American people need more qualified representatives to eliminate their grievous problems.

The problems of Spanish-speaking people of Texas are not adequately understood, from legal aspects, and to my knowledge there are no Spanish-speaking teachers in any Texas law schools. There is a need for lawyers, whether Spanish-speaking or not, to understand the problems.

Within the Spanish-speaking people in Texas and throughout the nation there is a tremendous shortage of persons of legal experience who are able to devote some of their time to those who are unable to secure counseling because of lack of finances.

One applicant had been a laborer, a machinist, and a policeman. He wrote: "As a police officer I learned many legal problems confronting Mexican Americans. I need legal training, perhaps to become a legal adviser to the police department."

Lionel Arron Pena, like many others, worked twenty hours a week during his early years in law school in Texas. Applying for an Opportunity Fellowship, he wrote: "I will return to my home country to engage in the general practice of law, where I will be confronted with a wide range of tasks, from serving income tax returns to servicing accused criminals." Five years later he was a senior partner in a law firm;

by the end of ten years he had been a city commissioner, acting mayor, chairman of the model city planning council, and active in other ways in the concerns of the community.

MEDICINE

Ten Mexican Americans have been partly supported by Opportunity Fellowships for degrees either as medical students or for postgraduate study. All of them came from the Southwest, and all but one are practicing there. Like the lawyers, they have become increasingly aware in the past decade of the importance of good professional care for the large population of Mexican Americans who are in economic need; and there has been a noticeable movement among the more recent applicants away from an interest in studying at the big eastern medical schools and toward study in the Southwest. A number of them have pointed out that the University of New Mexico Medical School has been developing its training program with the needs of the Mexican American population in mind. Several recent medical applicants have chosen to attend this medical school because they have an opportunity early in their studies to work in the barrios, to combine their theoretical studies with actual work with patients.

Almost without exception, others involved in medical sciences—public health nursing, medical social work, dentistry —take on themselves the double task, beyond the practice of their profession, of working to improve health standards of their people, and to educate the Anglo community to some of the facts of Mexican American life and custom it needs to have if Anglos also are to serve this public.

OTHER PROFESSIONS

The Mexican American Opportunity Fellows are active on all levels of academic life, as indicated here, and one of their functions in the universities is to help spark the changes being made in the teaching of history and the social sciences generally and to take more adequate account of the part of the Mexican Americans in the past and present life of the country. This function of the intellectuals is also pointed out in the chapter on the black Opportunity Fellows, and a better understanding of the history of the Mexican Americans will be equally significant for education generally.

Opportunity Fellows in other fields have been involved in political activities, several of them with Cesar Chavez, some serving La Raza in a variety of capacities. One lawyer, after ten years of law practice, is taking on the directorship of the Texas office of the Mexican-American Legal Defense and Education Fund, in which attorneys and others will work on litigation in the interest of Mexican Americans.

We find also Mexican American Fellows directing their interests toward the community—an architect is working at improving housing in the barrios, a city planner is working on community development programs for Spanish-speaking organizations in his community.

Chapter 4

THE PUERTO RICANS

In the previous chapter it was pointed out that there are large concentrations of Mexican Americans in several parts of the country, around Chicago, for instance, as well as around Los Angeles. For purposes of that account, however, the Mexican Americans from the Southwest—Texas, California, New Mexico, Arizona, Colorado—are central because there they have become most visible over the years; there they are nearer their roots and there the claims to land and power have become strongest. Most of the Opportunity Fellowship applications of the Mexican Americans came from these states and most fellowships were awarded there.

WHO THEY WERE

The Puerto Ricans, the other group of Spanish-speaking Americans, are much more concentrated. Over 600,000 of the 900,000 Puerto Ricans on the mainland listed in the United States census of 1960 lived in New York City, and the number has grown greatly since then. Nearly 30,000 more lived in the environs of New York, mainly in New Jersey. While Chicago had 32,000 and Philadelphia 14,500, no other city in the country had more than 6,000. In the last decade the entrance of Puerto Ricans into the schools of New York City has been a critical factor in the increasingly urgent need to change the educational design of our schools, and their entrance into the labor market is a critical factor there.

Forty-four Puerto Ricans had Opportunity Fellowships. About half applied from the Island, and almost all the rest from New York City. Some of those from New York were born there; most of them came to the city as children and went to the New York public schools.

THEIR EDUCATION

Though they came from both island and mainland, these Fellows were more homogeneous than other groups in their pre-fellowship education and experience. Twenty of the forty-four took their undergraduate work at the University of Puerto Rico, sixteen in New York City; four had no college degrees (these were painters and photographers), and four had been undergraduates in institutions outside of New York City.

Fourteen of the sixteen who had attended undergraduate colleges in New York stayed there for graduate work. However, only three of the twenty who had taken their undergraduate work in Puerto Rico came to New York City institutions for graduate study; five went to Chicago, three to Harvard, two to Yale, and one each to other universities in the East and the Midwest.

Of the Opportunity Fellows who came from the Island to study on the fellowship, very few remained in New York or elsewhere on the mainland. Almost all of them originally planned to return to Puerto Rico when they had finished their studies, and most of them did. Many, as the account of their careers indicates, have worked principally on the Island, with occasional or part-time activities in or around New York.

A report of 1971 shows seventeen of the forty-four Opportunity Fellows to be teaching at the University of Puerto Rico, most of them as regular faculty members, a few as lecturers. This group includes fourteen of the twenty who left Puerto Rico for graduate study on the fellowship; the other three graduated from universities in New York City. Ten of the seventeen have taken the Ph.D. degree, four have Master's degrees, one was on leave in 1970–71 pursuing her Ph.D. in the States. They studied mainly social sciences—political science, economics, history, social psychology, and anthropology. One is director of graduate studies in the education faculty of the University of Puerto Rico; another a professor in the law school. One, who has worked mainly in New York but has taught briefly in Puerto Rico, has a social work degree.

They have all taken their advanced degrees at major universities—Harvard, Yale, London University, Columbia, Chicago; one at Michigan State, one at Loyola, and one law professor at the university took his Ph.D. in Munich.

As most of the Puerto Rican Opportunity Fellows from the Island returned home when they had finished their studies, so most of the New York Fellows remained in New York City. Our records show only six of them working elsewhere —two teach at Howard University, one at Western Reserve, one at MIT. One is working for a Puerto Rican company in Honduras, and one is working in the Chapel Hill Hospital and teaching in North Carolina.

Most of the New York Puerto Ricans have been in social work, or have worked in organizations concerned with the welfare of Puerto Ricans on the mainland. Five are in community organization. Two have been active on New York City boards of education. One doctor is practicing in the city, and the two photographers, the one writer, and the painter who received fellowships all live and work in New York.

THE FELLOWSHIPS

TEACHING

We come to know, more and more surely, that many of the problems of the poor and deprived will not be solved without drastic changes in the education of children. Judgments made in schools about the ability of minority children have often been based on their performance with learning materials and on tests that were originally devised for an entirely different population. The accuracy of these judgments is to be doubted, not only when non-Anglo and Anglo children are compared, but also when poor children are compared with middle-class or upper middle-class children of whatever ethnic origin. In fact, for children who have been brought up in an environment and with customs, values, family patterns, and patterns of growth conspicuously different from those we have looked on as "normal" in American society, judgments of ability require a different kind of measurement.

Ada Elsa Izcoa graduated from the University of Puerto

Rico and went on to a Master's degree in psychology at the University of Iowa. She became director of the Evaluation and Guidance Office of the elementary and secondary schools of the College of Education of the University of Puerto Rico. She wrote:

> I had to cope with the situation that there was an inadequate number of tests, and even those gave questionable results. . . . In the testing field it is a basic concept that the norms for a test should be obtained on a representative sample of the population on which the test is to be used. This is not done in Puerto Rico. . . . However, if we look at the testing problem in Puerto Rico from a long-range perspective, doing basic research which will give us information about new techniques to study mental processes is of even more importance than obtaining norms, or validating tests.

A letter from a University of Minnesota sponsor of Miss Izcoa, distinguished for his work in the field of evaluation and his concern with learning, supported her conviction:

> There is not the slightest question but that a much more thorough, competent, and exact development of tests appropriate to individuals in (the Puerto Rican) culture is desperately needed as a foundation for guidance and, indeed, all of education. It is shocking to see the careless way in which American standardized tests are used by partly trained counselors in the schools. This, obviously, is not in the best interests of the Puerto Rican children.

Miss Izcoa, on an Opportunity Fellowship, took her Ph.D. at Loyola University, working with the professor who had first led her to an understanding of what was needed. She is now director of graduate studies in the School of Education in the University of Puerto Rico, where she is trying to revise existing programs and stimulate new ones that will provide the kind of academic, laboratory, and field experiences important for helping students meet through the schools the current needs of a growing society.

Jose Ferrer-Canales, an early Opportunity Fellow, has taught both in the States and in Puerto Rico. Now a professor of Spanish at the University of Puerto Rico, he has written widely—articles, essays, reviews—and had a varied teaching career before returning to Puerto Rico. He went to the University of Mexico on his fellowship and took his Ph.D. there, having already taught several years in Puerto Rico and in the States. He left a teaching post at Dillard University when he received the fellowship, taught at Texas Southern and Howard University after his degree; then he returned to Puerto Rico.

SOCIAL WORK

Eduardo Seda-Bonilla came to New York for graduate study. The direction of his studies was prompted by his own experience in watching a rural community of small farmers disappear with the beginning of sugarcane planting on an industrial basis. The small farms were consolidated, the tenants becoming wage earners or, more often, moving to the cities. He wrote:

> A scholarship from the University of Puerto Rico brought me to New York, where I met an organized neighborhood constituted mostly of people from my home community. This was their last attempt to recreate what they had lost. Most of them had given up already, and more and more were doing so every day under the requirements of the urban industrial society. The city does not like their un-city-like behavior, and they are giving up.

His two-year Opportunity Fellowship financed his principal work as a graduate student—a study made under the joint jurisdiction of Columbia University and the Payne Whitney Clinic, of the acculturation of the Puerto Rican family. It dealt with the issues that had been of concern to him from the time he first watched the breakup of a functioning small community. This research was part of a large study by psychiatrists, sociologists, anthropologists, and social workers, sponsored by Cornell Medical College and the Payne Whitney Clinic, which was seeking the social factors that make for mental disturbance in people of different cultural backgrounds. Mr. Seda-Bonilla's part of the study was of serious personal significance to him; it was in itself an important academic achievement; and it dealt with a social issue critical not only for the New York City population but also for the people of Puerto Rico, to whom he returned as a professor of anthropology at the university. He has had a distinguished career as a research director, consultant on educational projects, and visiting professor in most universities in the New York area.

Antonia Pantoja has had one of the most active careers among the Puerto Rican Fellows—one of the people who, having worked on a nonprofessional level, saw that she needed professional training in her field. Born in Puerto Rico, she took a normal-school diploma at the university and taught in the elementary schools. After several years of this, she came to New York and found a job with a community center, where she served as an untrained group worker with children and teenagers and reports: "The experience at the 110th Street Center was an unforgettable one, and one which opened to me avenues of inexhaustible possibilities. It was the immediate cause of my returning to school, and proved to me the potentialities in the field."

With the normal-school diploma she had earned ten years earlier, she entered Hunter College and completed her college studies in 1952, studying part time, working part time, and receiving small scholarship grants to help.

She was accepted at the New York School of Social Work, which she could enter only by enrolling for full-time study. That first year, in addition to her studies she worked at the Bethlehem Day Nursery as a liaison person between the nursery and the Spanish-speaking parents.

During her second year of study an Opportunity Fellowship made it possible for her to give all her attention to her schooling. As her field project that year, she worked at the Hudson

Guild in the Chelsea district of New York. She was to "develop relations among the Irish, Jewish, Greek, and Italian old residents of the area and the newcomers, Puerto Ricans and Negroes. This was done by organizing a housing clinic and a neighbors' committee to improve the area by working on common problems."

This matter of the relations between Puerto Ricans and the larger community within which they exist has continued to be a central interest throughout her professional career as director of the Community Relations Division of the Commission on Intergroup Relations of the City of New York and organizer of *Aspira*, the honor society for Puerto Rican students that seeks out and helps able young Puerto Ricans. She became director of the Puerto Rican Community Development Project for the Puerto Rican Forum, and later became executive vice president of the Forum. At this point her teaching career began. At the Center for New York City Affairs of the New School for Social Research she taught a course in community organization, with emphasis on the Puerto Ricans, and the next year was appointed to the Columbia University School of Social Work to teach a similar course.

She spent a year in Puerto Rico, teaching and working with a social action agency, and returned to the States to become in 1971 the executive director of the Puerto Rican Research and Resources Center in Washington.

Maria Canino, a more recent Opportunity Fellow, born in New York, writes of the fellowship that it has been one of the most important factors in her career: "It permitted me to begin graduate studies in social work, which would have been delayed for financial reasons had it not been for the Fellowship." She made swift and good use of her studies. Just five years after she completed them she became an associate professor and director of Puerto Rican studies at the new Livingston Colleges of Rutgers University, an experimental branch of the university which is designed for inner-city students. Actively involved in Puerto Rican affairs of New York, she has also been appointed to the Board of Higher Education of New York City.

PUBLIC AFFAIRS

Several Opportunity Fellows have been important in Puerto Rico during the industrialization of the Island in the 1950s and 1960s. Two of them are Carlos Lastra-Gonzalez, in his post as secretary of commerce, and Jenaro Baquero, now professor of economics at the university. Baquero, after taking a degree at the University of Puerto Rico, applied for an Opportunity Fellowship:

> Puerto Rico is in the process of solving some of the many economic and social problems the Island is confronted with. But in the meantime, many new very complicated ones are coming to the fore. That circumstance creates a need for well-qualified public professionals as well as for a continuous and dynamic program of social research.

Returning to Puerto Rico after two years at Harvard he worked at the Social Science Research Center of the university for several years and became economic consultant to the Legislative Assembly. In 1965 he was appointed secretary of commerce, a post he held for four years. He is now president '.R.A.C. of ˙ ˙erto Rico and a member of the economics ıty of the ˙ versity.

Abimel Hernandez returned to Puerto Rico in 1959 where he taught at the university, became an associate member of the planning board and headed two state agencies responsible for promoting and financing cooperative societies. He has continued active in the cooperative movement and is now chairman of the Cooperative League of Puerto Rico and also heads a corporation that develops turnkey projects.

With few exceptions, the Fellows who went on to public careers in Puerto Rico originally came from there and returned there—and numbers of them have held important public posts.

Carlos Lastra-Gonzalez, like others in this group, by the time he applied for an Opportunity Fellowship had already determined the part he wanted to play in the life of Puerto

Rico. He had graduated with honors from the university and was a Ph.D. candidate at Harvard on a limited scholarship from his home university. He was older than the average graduate student and had a family to support.

He made a study of the textile industry in Puerto Rico for his dissertation, since many companies were moving to Puerto Rico because of the favorable tax situation. He was interested in the development of unionism, in improvement in the wage scale and in the possibility of new companies that might add 30,000 direct jobs and twice as many related indirect jobs. The University of Puerto Rico, the then secretary of commerce of Puerto Rico, the Harvard professors, all predicted for him a career important to his country. Having completed his degree, he was appointed to the faculty of the University of Puerto Rico. Within ten years of his Harvard stay he was appointed secretary of commerce by President Munoz-Marin, and went on to become secretary of state and vice governor. After his term he became professor of economics and chancellor at the Interamerican University of San German, and is at present professor of economics at the School of Public Health of the University of Puerto Rico.

URBAN PLANNING

Carlos Lavendero also took his graduate work at Harvard, receiving Master's degrees in both city planning and landscape architecture. He had already served on the Puerto Rico Planning Board at the time of the fellowship. He took two degrees because of his conviction that appropriate planning involved knowledge of landscape architecture, and since his return to Puerto Rico he has worked in both fields.

LAW

John Carro took his law degree under the Opportunity Fellows program. From the time he entered college he was involved in the social problems of New York City. He served as a Department of Welfare investigator, a probation officer, and a street-gang worker with the City Youth Board. His aim was always to practice law in the Puerto Rican community in the city. After he achieved the law degree, by study-ing at the Brooklyn Law School at night, he continued working with the Youth Board:

> The work consists of co-ordinating a broad delin-quency prevention program to cope with the needs of our anti-social, delinquent youth. My role as a Supervisor is to supervise six workers who are attached to gangs of anti-social youngsters in an effort to channel their activities.

He also practiced law and worked with social agencies and Hispanic organizations concerned with civil rights and with providing legal counsel. He was appointed assistant to the mayor and, in 1969, a judge of the Criminal Court in New York.

Chapter 5

THE BLACKS

In all, 953 men and women were granted Opportunity Fellowships during the twenty-two year period of the program. Of these, nine forfeited the fellowship or died in the course of the year or shortly afterward, leaving 944 who carried through the terms of the grant and went on to further study or to work. Academic study accounts for 701 of them, and study in the visual or performing arts or writing accounts for 185.*

Of the 701 academic fellows, 342 or 48 percent were black; of the 185 Fellows in the arts, 142 or 77 percent were black. The arts fellowships are discussed in Chapter 10.

"THE BLACK EXPERIENCE"

One of the most dramatic—and controversial—events in education in the past five years has been the pressure for change in the curriculum of colleges and universities, and in ways of teaching in elementary and secondary schools, to bring studies relating to black people and other minorities into the educational system. This pressure has come primarily from the minority groups themselves, but administrators and teachers everywhere have responded and are increasingly aware of how remarkably we have ignored the study of the lives, experience, and history of black people, or Chicanos, or American Indians in our teaching. They are also becoming aware of how inadequately we have provided in our schools

*In addition, 58 Fellowships were awarded in 1971–1972. These figures are not included in the analysis of the figures.

for the children who have grown up with Spanish or an Indian language as their native tongue, and who come to schools where this critical fact is ignored.

Universities everywhere, from the most to the least innovative or distinguished, have suddenly included such studies in their curriculum. Their doing so has created anxiety and schisms, has opened up new possibilities for both teachers and students, and will affect the teaching of literature, the social sciences, and the arts for all time. At the same time, history is being rewritten to take account of the role of the blacks and other minorities in the development of our country, and the history books will never be the same.

Deans and department heads have been struggling and snatching to find men and women able to design such programs; and everybody concerned with the matter has discovered how ill prepared we are to deal with these newcomers to the curriculum because there are too few people well enough informed to design such programs or to teach the courses that have to be provided.

A history of this educational movement has no place here, but it is worth recording that many Opportunity Fellows are participating in it. The scholars of the Opportunity Fellowship generation are sophisticated and articulate about what is needed, and some of the most creative men and women involved in the effort have been Opportunity Fellows.

Among the black men and women who received fellowships in the academic fields mentioned above, teaching and research in the field of ethnic studies were reported by over 60 of the 325 who responded in the last quarter of 1970 to inquiries about their current work. The range of these activities can only be sampled here.

It will be the quality of the work of trained and committed scholars that will give ethnic studies the stature they must have. In the large field of studies relating to black people and black culture, some of the most distinguished names are those of Opportunity Fellows. For example:

Elliott Skinner, now Franz Boas Professor of anthropology at Columbia University, has been involved not only in his scholarly concerns with African culture but also in a variety of practical experiences with the life of Africa. He has led groups under the sponsorship of Operation Crossroads Africa to the Ivory Coast and to Upper Volta and has served on their board; he has been ambassador to Upper Volta. He taught African ethnology—courses on peoples and cultures and comparative institutions—seminars on urban development, on African political systems, and on modern political change; and wrote widely on African subjects before the African studies boom.

Charles Hamilton, political scientist, holds a chair in urban studies at Columbia University. He is currently writing on the development and transitions of the black political struggle and on the roles of the black preacher in social change. With Stokely Carmichael he wrote *Black Power: The Politics of Liberation in America,* and most recently he has published *The Black Experience in American Politics.* He is an active participant in affairs relating to black people.

C. Eric Lincoln, now professor of sociology and religion at Union Theological Seminary, has been very prolific and effective as teacher, writer, and lecturer in the fields of religion, sociology, and letters that relate to black people. He is editing a comprehensive series of books that will cover the entire black religious experience in the United States, is past president of the American Forum for International Study, which conducts summer programs in African studies for Americans in African universities, and is founder and president of the Black Academy of Arts and Letters, a society, he writes, "which strives to bring proper attention and acclaim to black scholars and artists, and which sponsors a variety of programs to aid and encourage aspiring Black Youth in Arts and Letters." He was recently elected to the American Academy of Arts and Sciences.

Martin Kilson, professor of political science at Harvard, has been visiting professor in the Institute of African Studies at the University of Ghana, has written *Political Change in a West African State* and *Apropos of Africa—Sentiments of American Negroes toward Africa,* has contributed widely to journals on political, educational, and social issues, and is central to the black studies program at Harvard.

Nathan Huggins, professor of history at Columbia, edited, with Dr. Kilson and Daniel Fox, *Key Issues in the Afro-American Experience*. He is a Guggenheim Fellow for 1971–72.

These are men who, through their research and scholarship, their participation in the reorganization of ideas about the place of black culture in the world's experience, will help the academic community and others to improve education in these respects.

Other Opportunity Fellows are teaching in these fields, working directly at the problems of curriculum change, and participating in studies, conferences, and workshops. These black professors are working in many ways to improve understanding of the black experience among black and white students alike, at community colleges in Detroit, North Carolina, New York City; at St. Louis University, Notre Dame, Morgan State, Virginia State College, the University of Wisconsin, Morehouse College; and in other places. For example:

At the University of Denver, Tilden LeMelle, professor of international relations, helped set up a fellowship program for Afro-American faculty of predominantly black colleges, and is teaching a course in Black Politics at the university.

At the University of Connecticut, Professor Floyd Bass is director of its Center for Black Studies; and is working for the Southern Regional Board on a study of black colleges, especially the teacher training and social service training they give, and their preparation for careers in southern politics and in foreign service. A political science professor at MIT, Willard R. Johnson, is chairman of the board of the New England Development Corporation and The Circle, Inc., a community-controlled corporation which promotes economic growth in black communities. A Howard University professor is consultant to a committee revising the social studies program of the Baltimore public schools to include materials relating to blacks and other ethnic minorities, and is teaching public school teachers in this field; a director of SEEK at Baruch College, in the City University of New York, is chairman of compensatory programs there; an English professor at Morgan State College is participating in the Negro Studies Syllabus project sponsored by the Ford Foundation there; an administrator at Bronx College is coordinator of its black and Puerto Rican studies.

THE FELLOWSHIPS

Thirty-nine of the academic fellows were still in graduate school when we heard from them—mainly men and women who were awarded fellowships between 1968 and 1971. Of the 303 who had completed their studies, 126, or 41 percent, entered college or university teaching. Recent information about 105 of these tells us that they are still in academic life, some now in administrative posts. Many of them are active in scholarship relating to the history of black people and in new curriculum planning that is concerned with the lives of black people.

After college, the largest number of the academic black Opportunity Fellows have gone into law—about 20 percent are either in law school now or are practicing law. Neither the social science professors nor the lawyers have limited their activities to the practice of their professions—the record indicates that a large proportion of them is engaged in public affairs.

LAW

The number of black applicants for law studies grew conspicuously in the second decade of the fellowships, and the quality of applicants in this field improved. It is obvious that many of the most able black students have been looking to the law as a profession that would be increasingly important for black people. As a result, about twice as many fellowships were awarded to black law students in the 1960s as in the 1950s.

One does not know, since the records tell little, what all the difficulties were that these men met in practicing law because they were black, but several of them pointed out that opportunities for being associated with good "white" law firms were slim; some of them sought careers in government and have remained there. Others found their way to careers in business after experience in government.

Many have worked for the government. Ulric Haynes, with

a B.A. from Amherst, took a law degree at Yale. As a law student he did legal work for the NAACP, and after his degree went to work for Governor Averell Harriman as executive assistant to the New York State Department of Commerce. He later served the United Nations in Geneva, the Ford Foundation in Africa, the Department of State as a specialist in African affairs, and on President Johnson's staff at the National Security Council. He is now vice president for public institutional affairs at Spencer Stuart & Associates, managerial consultants.

One of the earliest fellows in law, Alexander Farrelly, used his fellowship to obtain a law degree at Yale; he returned ten years later for a Master of Laws degree. He became a Caribbean Area specialist, and after the second law degree was appointed assistant U.S. attorney for the Virgin Islands.

Other lawyers have combined private practice, teaching, and civil rights work; one is involved in the improvement of schools in New York City to which mainly black children go.

Most of the men and women whose Opportunity Fellowships provided a year (sometimes two) of law school study, were more interested in studying public law than private or business law. But the character of that interest ranged widely. Cases from a sample of about 20 percent of the fellowships in law, chosen at random, will illustrate that range. For instance, a second-year law student, James N. Finney (1964–65), said:

> I intend to concentrate on Constitutional Law. With this training I hope to make some meaningful contribution to the civil rights struggle of American minorities. The law has been shown to be an effective weapon by which improvements can be brought about, and I believe that as long as gains can be made legally the forces of illegality and violence will be unable to gain an effective following.

This student had already demonstrated the character of his interest. He had been the student director, between his first and second years at law school, of a Harlem neighborhood

68

legal assistance project, and an intern during his first year at law school in the legal department of CORE, and he had presented a paper at a HEW conference, "Extension of Legal Services to the Poor."

Another student, Clarence Dilday (1966–67), born and brought up in Boston, an undergraduate at Howard, entered his third year of law school with a fellowship. He wrote when he applied:

> I would like to participate in the Voluntary Defender Program in the Roxbury District Court during my third year at school. Selected third year students are permitted to represent indigent defendants in the Roxbury District Court during their tenure in this program, which combines intensive classroom work with actual trial experience.
>
> I have been a lifelong resident of the Roxbury-Dorchester area.... This past summer I worked for Action for Boston Community Development, Inc., one of the sponsors of this program. My job as sub-area supervisor consisted of supervising children ages 14–16 in a general clean-up of vacant lots and streets in the Roxbury-Dorchester area and assisting them in their Model City Government of which I was co-adviser. I tutored children in Negro history and current events.
>
> My experiences have given me some insight into the problems that plague the members of my community which would make the legal services I could render much more valuable.

A professor at the Yale Law School describes the work of a second-year law student:

> The discussions we have had about program seem to me to represent intelligent and thoughtful selections of courses and seminars for a Black lawyer. In addition to his formal school work he has been an active participant on the *Law Journal*, for which he has recently published a comment; and he is organizing a Black Legal Research

Center to act as a research resource for the legal problems of Black communities.... These programs are especially valuable because they recognize the need for good lawyering and not just good intentions as the method for improving the status of poor people.... This man is one of our best students, Black or white. In a high-powered intellectual community, he more than holds his own.

Some of the law students saw the law as an instrument of social justice that includes but goes beyond the question of racial discrimination. One of them stated his expectations as follows:

The changing needs of the nation in foreign relations require a new and different kind of diplomat. The training provided by this program equips the graduate with skills far superior to those formerly brought to the diplomatic corps by those who sought foreign service as a mark of prestige. Completion of this program would also be a step toward a much needed increase in the supply of Black diplomats in the service of a nation founded on the principle of equality of opportunity.

One of the most distinguished holders of an Opportunity Fellowship in law is Leon Higginbotham, now a judge of a federal court in Pennsylvania. After having gone to a segregated school in New Jersey, where his best work was in mathematics and the physical sciences, he enrolled at Purdue University to study electrical engineering:

While at Purdue [this was in 1944–45] I was on a campus which then had segregated dormitories and in a community which denied Negroes equal access to public places of accommodation. I was then beginning to realize that the walls of segregation were vulnerable if rational methods of attack were used. I felt a strong moral obligation to choose a profession which would prepare me for the systematic destruction of racial and religious discrimination.

Though I originally chose law because of a vital concern about racial discrimination, I have kept law as my intended profession because it has potentialities which go beyond the eradication of racial injustices. I now see the potentialities of an intelligently formed international law which can partially weld unity among the nations of the world. I have found from practical experience in labor relations that reasonable legislation and arbitration can aid in amicably blending together the interests of management and labor. I do not believe that law, per se, is a panacea. I do believe however that it has given me effective tools which I may use for numerous public purposes whether I sit as a member of a Board of Education, a Board of Trade, or an NAACP Board of Directors.

Opportunity Fellows among black people have engaged in a wide range of activities in the interest of Blacks.

Marion Wright Edelman headed the Mississippi office of the Legal Defense Fund for NAACP at the time she reported, and was a practicing attorney in Jackson, Mississippi. At the present time she is director of the Center for Law and Education at Harvard University, and as the first woman to be elected to the Yale Corporation will find there new scope for her concerns.

Eleanor Holmes Norton served as law clerk to Judge Higginbotham after taking her degree, worked with the Mississippi staff of the Student Nonviolent Coordinating Committee during the summer, and then went on to be assistant legal director of the American Civil Liberties Union in New York. She is now chairman of the Commission on Human Rights of New York City.

Sheila Anne Rush worked with the NAACP Legal Defense Fund, handling cases of housing discrimination and violations of federal regulations having to do with urban renewal. She moved to Harlem to join the Architects Renewal Committee, a community planning group there.

James Albert Thomas worked with the Civil Rights Division of the Department of Justice. He then served as executive director of the Iowa Civil Rights Commission, as liaison officer with the Equal Employment Opportunity Commission in Washington and co-counsel for the Sub-committee on Administrative Practices and Procedure of the U.S. Senate Judiciary Committee. He is currently associate dean of the Yale Law School.

John W. Hatch, working for a large law firm in Chicago, serves in free legal advice clinics for indigent persons.

POLITICAL SCIENCE AND ECONOMICS

After law, the largest number of Opportunity Fellowships given to blacks in academic fields went to applicants interested in political science. Some have, since their graduate school days, been involved in international studies and activities. Martin Kilson's work at Harvard was on political development in Africa; two years after his Opportunity Fellowship he went to Sierra Leone under a grant from the Ford Foundation and has been active in African studies since. David Stratmon made a study of the Public Health Mission to Liberia for his Ph.D., went into government service, and fifteen years later was the deputy public affairs officer in the American Embassy in Paris. Other political scientists have written on Senegalese socialism and on Camaroon reunification; two have worked in Ethiopia and the Ivory Coast.

Other political scientists—with more domestic interests—have worked on such subjects as leadership in a Negro ghetto; this study was concerned with the relation of Negro leaders to officials in the political system, as well as to the ghetto. Charles Hamilton, then in the middle of his Ph.D. studies at the University of Chicago, applied for a fellowship for the period when he would write his thesis, "The Federal Courts and the Right of Negroes to Vote." This completed, and published in the *Wisconsin Law Review*, he began his teaching at Rutgers on constitutional law and civil rights. Ever since that time his writing and teaching have been concerned with political power and black people. Among other things he is co-author of a book on black power; an article about him in the *New York Times* (April 14, 1968) was called "An Advocate of Black Power Defines It."

Among the small number of Fellows in economics, the most outstanding is Andrew Brimmer who worked on economic problems in both India and the Sudan, became assistant secretary of commerce and was appointed to the board of governors of the Federal Reserve System. He has taught at Harvard, Michigan State, and the University of Pennsylvania. But the center of his activities has been government service.

HISTORY

Most of the historians who held fellowships are now teaching in universities, and the research and writing of most of these involve the history of the black people. John Willis was interested in Islam, and used his fellowship to work at the School of Oriental and African Studies in London. He became an international relations officer for the Peace Corps in the African region, lectured on Islamic topics in the Centre of West African Studies at the University of Birmingham, and edited *Studies on the History of Islam in West Africa.* Edgar Toppin took his Ph.D. a year after his fellowship year, taught in several southern colleges, and wrote on the history of blacks between Reconstruction days and World War I. He published articles in magazines devoted to black affairs and was on the editorial board of the *Journal of Negro History.*

Nathan Huggins is a historian who, in addition to his career as teacher and writer, has been commissioner on the Massachusetts Teacher Corps Commission, president of the Museum of Afro-American History in Boston, and a board member of the Children's TV Workshop, which produces *Sesame Street.* In addition, he is prolific in research and writing on questions relating to "the black experience." He has written a book called *Protestants Against Poverty,* is co-author of *Key Issues in the Afro-American Experience* and author of *Harlem Renaissance.*

SOCIOLOGY AND ANTHROPOLOGY

The Opportunity Fellows in anthropology and sociology also tend to combine university teaching with public activities of various kinds, like the lawyers, the political scientists and, to a lesser extent, the historians.

James Blackwell, after taking a Ph.D. in sociology, served as a Peace Corps director in Africa and the Pacific, and as director of the Peace Corps Center at the University of Wisconsin. After his Ph.D. in sociology, Samuel Adams studied at the London School of Economics and the Maxwell School of Public Affairs of Syracuse University, served on economic missions to Indochina, Nigeria, Mali, and Morocco. He acted as U.S. representative to the fifth special session of the United Nations General Assembly, and was ambassador to the Republic of Niger. In 1969 he became assistant administrator, Bureau for Africa, Agency for International Development, Department of State.

Ubert Vincent, a sociologist, has participated since 1960 in antipoverty programs and is now general counselor in the State University of New York at the Brooklyn Urban Center.

The interests of the anthropologists range from South Asia, the Pacific Islands, Africa, South America, and Mexico to the study of blacks in the American South. Some of their research is in fields related to "the black experience"—the cultural development of Negro Africa, the interaction of ethnic groups in Guyana, and relations in the United States between Negroes and Indians. Almost all the anthropologists are active in the affairs of the black community in whatever part of the world their professional interests lie.

SOCIAL WORK

A small number of blacks held Opportunity Fellowships in social work. The range of activities can be illustrated by the work seven of them are doing, on whom we have recent information:

One is director of the social work program of Antioch College. One teaches social work and social research at Bryn Mawr College, is active in the Welfare Rights Organization movement, and is doing research in child development, especially in black urban areas.

One works with the Big Brother Residential Treatment Center for Adolescent Boys, dealing with individuals and families of emotionally disturbed adolescents. She is on the board of directors of the Association of Black Social Workers Day Care Center and Youth Service Center.

One is a second-year full-time student in the Social Work School at Wayne University, and editing its paper. He is also teaching Afro-American history and social studies at a local community college and in the public schools.

One is administrative assistant for community services at a New York hospital. He says: "My position might be considered both a community organization task and a public relations function—a vehicle of communication between the administration of the hospital and the community, which has many Black and Puerto Rican residents."

One, in addition to casework and group work, is involved in the Head Start program of her community.

The seventh, who received a social work degree in 1965 with the help of a fellowship, after doing case work in a public agency went on to work with the Child Service Association in New Jersey, was a psychiatric social worker with the Youth Development Clinic of Newark, and was consultant to Princeton University's cooperative school program.

Social workers, and sociologists, have served on community projects and in community problems; they have directed Head Start training programs, worked to bring housing specialists and the community together on housing projects, directed Haryou Act projects, and served on the planning committee for the White House Conference on Youth in Conflict.

Several people in these fields worked under Ford Foundation grants in the years following the completion of their graduate studies—one on a grant for African studies, another as a director of the Ford Inter-agency Project, a participant in the Ford Great Cities program.

LITERATURE AND LANGUAGE

Among the thirty Opportunity Fellows who were students of literature and language, about half were in English and half in Romance languages—French or Spanish. This is a high proportion of foreign-literature students. We do not find as many eminent scholars here as we do among the political scientists or lawyers, but their record of accomplishment as graduate students is high. Of those who had fellowships before 1965 and were going for the Ph.D., about two-thirds had achieved it by 1965. In 1965, with six exceptions, the thirty were teaching in colleges around the country, most of them in black colleges in the South; one was at Rutgers, one at Harvard, one at San Francisco State. Of the six exceptions, four were teaching in high schools (only one in the South), one was a librarian, and one has had a career of many parts—translator, director of African affairs for a chemical company, cultural attaché.

It is interesting to observe that most of the Ph.D. dissertations of this group, unlike those of the political scientists and historians, were on conventional doctoral subjects not concerned with literature by or about black people.

MEDICINE

About thirty-five black students received Opportunity Fellowships for medical studies. A review of their statements of intention at the time they applied, and of recent information about them, shows not only the high level of completion that we find in all fields but also a high correspondence between what they said they wanted to do and what they have done.

Slightly over half the fellowships in medicine were for study for the M.D. degree; the rest were for advanced study by men who already had their first medical degree. Of those who completed their studies more than three or four years ago, about two-thirds are both teaching and practicing medicine. Their teaching appointments range across the medical schools of the country—the University of Pennsylvania, the University of Michigan, Oklahoma, UCLA, Western Reserve. Their specialties include pediatrics, internal medicine, surgery, dermatology, and oral surgery, with perhaps more in surgery than in any other one field. The record shows a very small number in psychiatry.

The doctors are much less communicative about their interests in community or social aspects of medicine, either in their original applications or in their statements about their present activities, than are the medical men from other minority groups or blacks in other fields. However, one third-year medical student explains why he plans to go back to Bedford-Stuyvesant in Brooklyn, where he came from, to practice medicine:

> In the summer of 1968 I worked in a community health program in the central Brooklyn area that was sponsored by the Student Health Organization. This program attempted to deal with the varied health problems of large numbers of underprivileged people in our community. Health education, hospital administration, Medicare, and lead poisoning of children in substandard housing were some of the issues confronted. Having lived and grown up in Bedford-Stuyvesant I had always been aware of the lack of adequate medical facilities available. However, this summer's experience in community medicine has brought home the fact that very little is being done to improve the health conditions of these people. My life-long desire to work in my community to better the quality of health care was indeed strengthened by this summer's experience. After medical school I plan to train in general surgery; my experience in medicine combined with the knowledge of the way of life and the people should enable me to contribute to the general health and welfare of the community.

A fourth-year medical student planned to go into physical medicine and rehabilitation. He took a Bachelor's degree in 1939 with a major in science and mathematics; ten years later took a Master's degree in education, and three years after that entered medical school. He wrote:

> I hope to specialize in Physical Medicine and Rehabilitation, a field that has become increasingly important with each stride forward that Medicine takes. As far as I have been able to determine (from authorities in the field) there are no Negroes qualified or in training to accept responsibility in this specialty. Whether it

means pioneering or not, I wish to prepare myself to the point where I would be able to accept the challenge to build such a department, including a program of teaching and participation in research.

A woman applying for the fellowship for her second year in medical school writes:

> Since doctors are badly needed in my home, St. Thomas, V.I., I intend to return home to practice and to live. I would like to practice only in the hospital clinic as I think its patients are very often neglected, be it because of lack of personnel or lack of monetary compensation. By restricting myself to the clinic I believe that I could give it the time that it deserves and eliminate the temptation of concentrating on my private patients. I hope some day to be married and therefore am not as worried about monetary needs as a man must be. My community is badly in need of a person who is free to be open to the needy patient. The result of overworked doctors who split up their time is already evident. There is both indifference and resentment on the part of the less fortunate clinic patient toward the field of medicine.

Statements like these are not common. If the physicians are interested in the social aspects of medicine, one finds little evidence of it in the record. What we do find is evidence that most of these men and women are deeply involved in their professional lives—the list of their professional connections is long and impressive.

BIOLOGICAL AND PHYSICAL SCIENCES

Biologists and physical scientists among the blacks have been active in the educational affairs of black students, in recruitment of blacks for the study of science, and in research and action relating to problems of the poor and of the black poor. A professor of zoology, an early Opportunity Fellow, points out that with the reduction of state and federal support, financing graduate study will be increasingly serious for minority students. He points out that the major source of help within the universities is teaching fellowships, and that "by the nature of their background many of the minority students either are not qualified to teach in our undergraduate laboratories until they have done some remedial work, or they badly need to put all of their effort into course work and other aspects of their own training, at least for the first two or three years of graduate work." He writes that his own fellowship provided this freedom for him—like so many Opportunity Fellows, he had always had to work while studying. The critical issue is that the universities must try to increase the number of black students in science (which he is helping to do) at a time when their financing is becoming more difficult.

A microbiologist working in a commercial laboratory gives talks on drug abuse to community and business groups and to schools, and works with a Negro organization in which black junior and senior high school students spend a day with a black supervisor in various fields of social interest.

A professor of physics at the University of Minnesota recruits minority students to go to the university, advises the Afro-American Studies Department, and tutors black students in physics and mathematics. "The Opportunity Fellowship," he writes, "is often crucial in determining whether a disadvantaged student will continue his intellectual development to the point of creative study." A biology professor is adviser to the model cities program, to the Afro-American Society of his community, and to the Black Students Union.

A small number of men received Opportunity Fellowships to complete work for a Ph.D. in chemistry; all completed it, all did superior work and were elected to the major honorary societies, and all became research chemists. Several also teach. One geologist not only teaches but is also doing research on mineral resources in Canada. Most mathematicians are teaching.

Chapter 6

THE ORIENTAL AMERICANS

Opportunity Fellowships were granted to Oriental Americans from the beginning of the program until 1965. At that time a review of the applicants and of the opportunities that had been opening up for men and women of Far Eastern background made it clear that, although there was no question that applicants needed financial aid to complete their studies, their eligibility for conventional fellowships was in general greater than that of other groups the Foundation was interested in helping. The hardships men and women with Far Eastern background suffered during and immediately after World War II, the great need Japanese Americans had to catch up with the careers that had been interfered with by internment in the Relocation Centers, made fellowships important. Their capacity to profit from educational opportunities in the years that followed relieved the pressure on them, and the Foundation judged that students with Japanese, Chinese, and Korean background were better able to secure financing for their education than were the blacks, American Indians, and Spanish-speaking students. It was decided in 1965 to concentrate the limited funds of the Foundation where the need seemed greatest.

WHO THEY WERE

Most of the Oriental Opportunity Fellows were Japanese. There were many fewer Chinese, and only a handful of Koreans. Also, a large fraction of the grants went to men and women in the arts—thirty-two of the ninety-six fellowships awarded to Orientals in the fifteen years of that program. Those thirty-two are discussed in Chapter 10. Here we will review the sixty-four fellowships in academic fields—where in their educational lives they were when the fellowship was awarded, where they came from and where they went when they had completed their work, and the part they now play in the academic and intellectual life of the country.

Within the field of academic studies, the goals of the Oriental Fellows had more in common than the goals of other groups. There were fewer who wanted support for studies or other activities outside the more conventional academic disciplines. Within those disciplines, students were predominantly interested in the social sciences, and within the social sciences, more were interested, understandably, in comparative studies of governments and social institutions. Fellowships were frequent in political science, sociology, and international relations; there were some in history and a few in anthropology. Their interest in anthropology was in general like their interest in sociology and government, of a cross-cultural kind. There were few fellowships for literature or philosophy, none in mathematics or the physical sciences. Only six Fellows studied medicine, and of these, one turned to microbiology as leading more directly into research. Three students were given fellowships to complete already-begun law studies, and one to begin law at Yale, but after that first year he withdrew from the law school and entered for a Ph.D. in philosophy. He went on to teach philosophy at Yale and Fordham, and is now (1971) an associate professor of philosophy at the University of Texas, holding a fellowship for research and writing from the American Council of Learned Societies. Of the three who took law degrees, one went on to a Master's degree in business administration, entered business in Honolulu as a legal and administrative assistant, and is now vice president of the company.

As a group, the Oriental applicants were farther ahead in their graduate study than were others in the program. They were sophisticated; they had already carried their education quite far, often to the point of specialization, and in a number of cases the fellowship request was for postdoctoral study. With this head start toward professional life, it is not surprising that the record of their later activities is a very good one; fewer risks were taken in granting funds to these students than to some other groups, and their careers were more predictable. Their record of subsequent fellowships is high. Even when their studies turned their careers in directions they had not anticipated, as happened in five or six cases, success in the new venture was to be expected. The medical student turned microbiologist already had an excellent record at the Johns Hopkins University, where both her medical and her later studies were carried on. The law student turned philosopher after a year at law school was clearly an intellectually superior student.

THEIR EDUCATION

While many of the sixty-four Fellows being discussed were not from the continental United States, forty had been at mainland universities. A good many of these were second- or third-generation Americans. Their Bachelor's degrees were from universities in all parts of the country, mainly from large and well-known institutions, about half public and half private.

Three students had had their undergraduate work in Korea, Taiwan, or China; all three, however, had been in this country at least five years and were well on their way to their graduate degrees when they received Opportunity Fellowships.

Twenty-one of the academic fellowships went to students who came from Hawaii for graduate study, and they will be mentioned later.

The academic history of the mainland-educated Chinese and Japanese was not unlike that of other superior students, and, as the story of their subsequent careers indicates, the chief difference one finds is that their ethnic background, obviously a hurdle in many ways, also provided a large number of them with unique opportunities for teaching and other work. They used this fact of their lives in very constructive ways—useful to themselves and to fill an educational need in American higher education that grew more and more insistent in the years after World War II:

It is imperative that we understand in this country the true desires and aspirations of these people of the East. . . .

Strong discrimination has been implanted in the minds of young students by the stress of war-time propaganda. There is a tendency for these students to look upon the quaint side of Oriental life and not stop to analyze the logical sources of this quaintness. A sense of frustration could be seen in the question raised by a student, "Is it at all possible to understand them?"

This was written in 1953 when Noboru Inamoto was a graduate student of public law and government at Columbia. Subsequently he went twice on travel grants to Japan, to work at the National Diet Library. His teaching career has been at the University of Southern California, where he is in the Department of Asian Studies; and he spent 1970–71 on leave at Waseda University in Tokyo as resident director of the Year in Japan program of California's private universities and colleges. He was sponsor of the USC Asian Studies Society, which put on programs directed toward students and the community, and has compiled audiovisual material on the history and culture of Japan. He writes books on the Japanese language and teaches a course on the heritage, contributions, and problems of Japanese Americans; and for eleven years, in the hope of encouraging better understanding between Japanese and Americans, he has conducted educational study tours to Japan almost annually.

On many levels the Japanese American Opportunity Fellows are advancing the knowledge and understanding, of American students in universities, about Oriental history and culture and the relations of the Orient to the Western world, just as some of the most distinguished black scholars are advancing knowledge of the experience of black people in this country, and advancing their cultural and political role.

THE FELLOWSHIPS

LINGUISTICS

A dramatic story of a change of direction is the career of Lillian Yuriko Nakai. She applied for and was granted an Opportunity Fellowship to study at the Russian Institute at

Columbia University, the Far Eastern and Russian Institute at the University of Washington, or the School of Regional Studies at Radcliffe. Her analysis in her application of the course her studies would take at each of these was testimony to a thorough inquiry into their offerings. In each case her attention was on Russian studies:

> Hawaii, as the westernmost American territory of major educational, cultural and political activity, serving as a point of concentration in Occident–Orient exchange, will be further expanded along lines of inter-cultural matters, with the focal point at the University of Hawaii, which is already an educational center of repute. Thus, Russian area studies should be expanded here and I should like to be a contributing part of such a program.

She was one of the people whose studies had already taken them a long way—she had completed with honors the intensive intermediate Russian summer course at Georgetown University, on a Honolulu scholarship. For a large Buddhist organization she had done two translations from the French of technical articles, about which the person who commissioned them wrote: "your translation of Amkda... received wide acceptance. Your recent translation of *Bombai* has won countless praises from all corners of the world." Before that she had studied—on a Fulbright Act Fellowship—Russian, German, and Spanish, as well as continuing with French, at the University of Toulouse. At the time she applied to the Foundation she was taking linguistic courses at the University of Hawaii, and advanced readings in Russian. She pursued her Russian studies during the fellowship year but became more and more involved in linguistics. Since then she has done research on Lilliiet (a Salishan language of British Columbia), Tibetan, and Samoan, has run language programs for the Peace Corps for Thailand, Nepal, Gonga, and Samoa, and has written texts for several Philippine and Samoan dialects and has worked on a Japanese program for the Hawaii Department of Education. In early 1971 she was on her way from

84

Thailand to Honolulu where funds had been appropriated for her to complete a Samoan grammar.

The subject matter of this can't-stop-to-breathe career is rather exceptional among Oriental Fellows. But the intense intellectual purpose, talent, and persistence is a common phenomenon among them.

Opportunity Fellowships not only provided students with funds for completing studies already undertaken but often gave Fellows new opportunities for expanding professional careers already underway.

LIBRARY SCIENCE

Warren Michio Tsuneishi was a part-time graduate student in political science at Yale when he applied for a fellowship. To support his family of four he also worked full time at the Yale library. He was then head of the Oriental language section of the Catalogue Department, supervising the cataloguing of Japanese and Chinese works, and assisting with acquisitions. Three years after the Opportunity Fellowship he joined the Library-of Congress as head of the Far Eastern Languages Section of the Descriptive Cataloguing Division, and after his doctorate was granted in 1960 he returned to Yale as Curator of the East Asia Collections. He was appointed chief of the Orientalia Divisions of the Library of Congress in 1966.

The Opportunity Fellowship provided Dr. Tsuneishi with a year of freedom to study and to complete his course work without the pressure of a full-time job, and therefore with the opportunity to find larger possibilities for his special capacities and experience than might otherwise have come.

SOCIAL SCIENCES

Eugene S. Uyeki was far along in his graduate studies in sociology at the University of Chicago when he applied for the fellowship. This provided him the time to finish his research for his Ph.D. dissertation which was concerned with relating changes in self-concept to different social situations, a part of his interest in personality and social organization. A

85

year later he had his degree and was appointed to the faculty of Case Institute of Technology. Dr. Uyeki is at present provost of social and behavioral sciences at Case Western Reserve University.

There were four social work Fellows, one in guidance and one in human relations. Three of the social work students were halfway through their training before applying for Opportunity Fellowships; the fourth, who had had all her previous education on the mainland, wanted to go to Hawaii for her degree, which she did. She worked for several years in Hawaii after her degree, then returned to California where she had originally lived, and worked there in a medical center. Two of the other social workers took posts with public agencies in California, and the fourth with the public schools of Concord, Massachusetts. The student who took a degree in guidance had had her undergraduate and her graduate study in Hawaii and went to the mainland for further training. She returned to Hawaii on a research project for the National Institute of Mental Health—a comparative study of psychological illnesses among Japanese patients in Japan and in Hawaii. It is hard to exaggerate the importance of comparative studies, with skills and insights learned in one area of study brought to another area, in relation to our present dilemmas, created by the increasingly vocal dissatisfaction with our total attitude, as a nation, to the past and present life of these groups.

The one Fellow who came with a Master's degree to work in the Center for Human Relations at New York University has been a probation officer in Los Angeles and has had a career mainly with the YWCA.

James Hirabayashi, an anthropologist, after five years at the University of Washington and a Fulbright Fellowship to Japan, wanted to study in the Department of Social Relations at Harvard. His research project was already established—he had spent his Fulbright year in a mountain village in Japan and in Tokyo libraries preparatory to making a comparative study of that community in relation to the norms of national values and behavior.

With an Opportunity Fellowship he completed his degree

and was appointed to the faculty of the San Francisco State College, where he is now professor of anthropology and dean of the School of Ethnic Studies. He has carried on research in Japan, Guam, Nigeria and Liberia and with Indian groups in North America and various ethnic groups in San Francisco.

TEACHING

College teaching and research are the most prominent occupations among the sixty-four academic Oriental Fellows. Our information about what they are doing is quite recent— for fifty-two of the sixty-four it is not older than five years, and for thirty-seven of these it is from 1971. This information shows that thirty-two of the sixty-four hold or have recently held faculty posts at universities and colleges—most of them in teaching, a number in administration, where they are typically directors of East Asian centers, deans of ethnic studies, or chairmen of Asian studies departments.

Of the thirty-two in the university group two teach literature, one bacteriology, one nursing, one philosophy, and four medicine or public health. But about three out of four are in the social sciences—Asian studies, history, political science, sociology, and anthropology. Some if not all of their teaching deals with political, historical, or cultural issues of Oriental life and thought or the relations between East and West.

There is less interest in teaching children than one finds among other Opportunity Fellows; although several Oriental Fellows are teaching in departments of education in universities, only three are teaching in public schools.

HISTORY

Ton Te-Kong had taught Chinese history at National Anhui University in China, left the country, and had to make his career here. He studied American history and at the time of his application had passed his comprehensive examinations, and his dissertation, "Diplomatic Relations between China and the United States between 1854 and 1860," was underway. For this he needed time and access to the National Archives in Washington and records in other libraries.

Minoru Shinoda was interested in the feudal period of Japanese history and had undertaken a translation from the Japanese of a five-year period of the principal historical compilation relating to the early part of the feudal period. He had completed a draft and needed a year to improve his translation, organize his notes, and write a critical analysis. Dr. Shinoda is now at the University of Hawaii, acting director of the Culture Learning Institute of the Far East Center.

MEDICINE, LAW, AND OTHER PROFESSIONS

Of the medical men and lawyers (as indicated earlier, the number is small), some are teaching; their choice of activities apparently has less "ethnic" orientation than is the case with other Opportunity Fellowship groups. It may be that pressure for improved medical and legal services is not so urgent as for other groups.

The four physicians and two lawyers who completed their degrees went into private practice or some combination of research and teaching. Two Fellows are in government service, three in research, one in Christian education, and one in city planning. Three are apparently still students.

STUDENTS FROM HAWAII

Twenty-one of the Oriental American students had taken their Bachelor of Arts degrees at the University of Hawaii, went to the mainland to study, and later received Opportunity Fellowships. Their experience was, obviously, somewhat different from that of the Orientals who had been born on the mainland or had lived there long enough to go through college.

Twelve of the twenty-one went to the mainland immediately on graduating from college in Hawaii; others went within two to five years after completing their undergraduate degrees; about four of them we don't know.

Most of them had had up to four years of study in mainland universities before they received Opportunity Fellowships— that is, they were well on the way toward their degrees (as was true of other Oriental American Opportunity Fellows).

About a third of them had from five to eight years of graduate study before the fellowship.

All but three completed the degree for which they were working when they became Fellows. In most cases this was the Ph.D.; in two cases a medical degree, in one a law degree, in two a social work degree, and in four a Master of Arts degree.

Eleven of the twenty-one returned to the Islands sooner or later, several making a number of return visits to the mainland to work for short times; and eight have made their careers on the mainland, although some of these have worked for a short time on the Islands. Of the eleven who returned to the Islands, six are teaching at the university, all of them active in the intellectual life of the university and the community. Two are in public health, two are doing research and writing, one is a business executive, and one a supervising teacher.

Of the eight who either did not go back, or went back and returned to the mainland, five are teaching in universities, two are surgeons, and one is an orthopedic dentist.

The Fellows having academic careers in Hawaii are active in matters that relate to Far Eastern studies. George Akita is professor of Japanese history. Shiro Amioko went home to take a place on the education faculty and become an associate dean at the University of Hawaii; he is now state superintendent of education for the State of Hawaii. Thomas Chang, immediately on his return to Hawaii, was appointed to head a special program for gifted children and is now teaching educational psychology at the university. Minora Shinoda is director of the Institute of Advanced Projects of the East–West Center at the University. George Yamamoto has studied and traveled in Japan since the fellowship year, and is on the sociology faculty of the University.

Agnes Niyekawa, after holding a postdoctoral fellowship of the New York State Psychiatric Institute for three years, returned to Hawaii to the university's Research and Development Center, and then went on to postdoctoral studies in linguistics at MIT.

Of the Fellows in academic life on the mainland who originally came from Hawaii, Frank Motofuji is professor of

Oriental languages at Berkeley; Stanley Kim started as a social worker, took his Ph.D. in social work and sociology, and taught at the Milwaukee School of Social Work of the University of Wisconsin, where he was involved in a Peace Corps training program. He is now on the faculty of the University of Michigan School of Social Work. Jas Irikura, on completing his degree, joined the Kent State faculty and is doing research on Japan and East Asia; Doris C. Ching is professor of education at California State in Los Angeles; and Lillian Kitaguchi Nishimura was appointed to the education faculty of Jersey City State College. In sum, except for the two surgeons (who do some teaching) and the one orthopedic dentist, all Hawaiian Opportunity Fellows on the mainland are, or were, on college or university faculties.

Chapter 7

THE
PACIFIC ISLAND TRUST
TERRITORIALS

Reviewing the Opportunity Fellowships to men in the Pacific Island Trust Territories after a review of fellowships to Japanese and Chinese students provides a dramatic illustration of the wide range of educational needs which the John Hay Whitney Foundation Program has tried to meet. Among Oriental Americans there is consistently high capacity for scholarship on an advanced level, interest and experience in research, the intention, the directed effort, and the achievements which put these students in positions of intellectual leadership. A drive for leadership is apparent also among the applicants from the Trust Territories, who seek training that will give them leadership in their local governments; they have the intention and the motivation for it, and a gratifying proportion of them have achieved it. The difference lies in their level of education and experience as they apply and move through the fellowship year and function afterward; their own comments about their work are the best evidence of their educational needs.

Twenty-six fellowships have gone to men from the Trust Territories; twelve of them now hold important posts in their governments—this was the object of their studies. One is a newspaper publisher; three are teaching in local schools; six are still students; only one failed to complete the full year of study. Three have fallen from sight in the past five years; we have knowledge of the current or fairly recent activities of the rest.

The earliest Trust Territory fellowships were granted in the early 1950s, but most of them date from the middle 1950s and early 1960s. At that time it was becoming increasingly clear that, if persons native to these Pacific Islands were to take over their government from the American administrators as had been mandated, people must be trained to the task. The applicants were at least as aware of this as their American governors.

WHO THEY WERE

Dwight Heine, now a special consultant to the High Commissioner of Saipan in the Mariana Islands, who holds the rank of cabinet minister, had an Opportunity Fellowship in 1958–59. Ten years earlier he had been superintendent of the elementary schools, and the year before the fellowship he had served as district educational administrator of the Marshalls District. Two years after his return from studying, he became president of the Marshall Islands Congress, and in 1965 he was appointed district administrator of the Marshall Islands, the first and only Micronesian to hold such high office until 1970, when three other Micronesians were appointed.

What he sought in the fellowship was a means to a college degree, which had become a necessary qualification in the position he was then holding. He speaks of himself as having been, in 1948, the first Micronesian to go to an institution of higher learning. He had received a scholarship jointly sponsored by the University of Hawaii and the United States Navy and was admitted to the university as an unclassified student. His education prior to that had been in the mission schools in the Marshalls and the Carolines. "English was taught in these schools as a foreign language," he writes, "and limited to one hour a week, as the Japanese authorities would not permit the extension of its teaching."

But he had a job with the navy during the war as interpreter, translator, and adviser on the area, and he learned English that way. After this experience he became superintendent of elementary education and from that point on his education was advanced in many ways. The United Nations sent him to study in New Zealand, Samoa, and Fiji, and on his return he was appointed district educational administrator. As he moved ahead the need for academic training became increasingly urgent. He returned to the University of Hawaii as a junior under a scholarship from the Trust Territory government, and then needed support for his final year. This the Opportunity Fellowship provided.

He writes of the need in the Islands for educated young people, and the difficulty of getting and keeping teachers: "Whenever a teacher has acquired enough training to do a good job, the attractions from other jobs pull him away." These problems were voiced by most of the other Fellows, whose education during that decade was moving far ahead of the education of their contemporaries, and Heine's story is a symptom of the situation these men are trying to deal with.

John Avila Mangefel of Yap is now a member of the Congress of Micronesia. His chief concern, when he applied for a fellowship, was to get experience in writing. He was at the University of Hawaii:

> If I am granted a fellowship I will take one or two courses in writing at the University and spend the rest of my time actually writing and have the benefit of criticism and comment on my work.... In Yap I have tried to write but found myself in some difficulties due to various things. The environment was not favorable, especially for an amateur writer: there was no place where I could go and do research. There was no library at all; no expert person or persons in this field to whom I could turn for advice. In addition the homes in Yap lack electricity which makes it hard to work at night. I found myself in frustration because I lack all these things....
>
> I have lived through the Japanese administration, and now the American in Yap. Within this period, I have seen some great changes over my people; and I myself have gone through some great change. So far, nobody has done any work on these changes and I feel that it is important to put them in writing before other changes take place.

Like most of the Trust Territory Fellows, he moved into political activity almost as soon as he returned home.

> The Congress is a full-time business. When we are not in session I serve as Consultant to the Yapese people in all aspects of our development. I devote my time to political education on our future political status. Before I became a member of Congress I was Superintendent of Education in the Yap District. I feel now, as a Congressman, that I am much more helpful to my people as well as the people throughout the whole Trust Territory of the Pacific Islands.

The importance the American Indians and the Mexican Americans feel of maintaining and nourishing their ancient culture as they become more involved in the dominant patterns of American life is paralleled by the concerns of men like Mangefel.

"Through the influence of western civilization, American Samoa, my birthplace, is undergoing change." This is Peter Coleman speaking, one of the earliest Opportunity Fellows from the Islands, who took a degree at Georgetown Law School, after the fellowship. He goes on:

> In view of this changing condition, which is likely to go much further as time goes on, the objective of my education is to conserve the best of Samoan culture and at the same time to acquaint the Samoan people with the great intellectual tools, social concepts and institutions of the West so that the Samoans may maintain respect for their native heritage and skill in their traditional arts and crafts, but at the same time may learn to meet on equal terms with other peoples the conditions of the modern world.

He pointed out that the Samoans had never had a civil form of government, but would be expected to when American Samoa moved out of the control of the United States Navy. He took law for his field because of the importance of setting up a legal system that will consider what constitutes justice in the light of Samoan tradition and customs. What is needed is "a judicial process based on moral and legal principles of Western civilization merged with communal justice perpetuated by the Matai System of American Samoa" (a chief or Matai heads each family). This is exactly the reason given by a number of American Indians who have asked for Opportunity Fellowships for the study of law.

Four years after he took his law degree, Coleman was governor of American Samoa, and the first constitution of American Samoa was adopted during his term. Five years after that he went on to serve as district administrator of the Mariana Islands and since 1969 has been deputy high commissioner of the Territory of the Pacific Islands.

In all groups some Opportunity Fellowships were awarded to give the applicants training for work they were already engaged in. The need for such awards was particularly obvious in the Trust Territories. The effort, their own and the American government's, to place Islanders in positions of importance made it necessary that men take government posts before they had the educational qualifications. So a large proportion of the applicants needed training for jobs they already held—as Dwight Heine did. Ermes Siales, of the Caroline Islands, had been involved in community development, as an apprentice. He was granted a fellowship for 1961–62 to study community development in the Philippines. Two years later, on his return from his studies, he was appointed community development officer for the Truk territorial government. He had responsibility for implementing programs that "aim at strengthening self-reliance, adaptability and effective planning capability of communities, social institutions and individuals. The main programs are in infrastructures and human resource development."

Other men involved in government affairs, by election or appointment, are Charles T. Domnick, who spent his Opportunity Fellowship year at the University of Hawaii and, as of 1971, is a member of the House of Representatives of the Congress of Micronesia, having had in 1970 a term at the College of Public Administration at the University of the Philippines.

John S. Tarkong, of the Carolines, had a B.A. from Northland College in Ashland, Wisconsin, and was given a fellowship to study law. He is now legal research analyst in the office of the Legislative Counsel of the Congress of Micronesia.

Mitsuo Solang took a B.A. at the College of Guam in 1965 and that year received a fellowship for a year of graduate study in sociology. Granted an additional fellowship year by his government, he completed an M.A. in sociology. He is now district director of public affairs in the office of the administrator of the Palau District.

David Ramarui took his Bachelor's degree at the University of Hawaii, an Opportunity Fellowship taking him through the final year. He was an administrator for the Department of Education of Palau, became a senator in the Micronesian Congress, and returned to academic life as deputy director of education.

Men who are more recent Fellows and are still studying, plan, like those before them, to go back to their home islands. We have record of only one who has remained in the States.

One Opportunity Fellowship was given in the field of public health. Lorenzo Iriarte, of Guam, had a high school diploma. In the United States Navy he took a course for medical assistants, reported by the HEW official who recommended him to be a rigorous and demanding course. Through the Opportunity Fellowship, Iriarte was able to attend the Johns Hopkins School of Public Health, where he was granted a Master of Public Health degree. At the time there was not a single person with specialized training in this field in Guam, an important military base for the United States. Mr. Iriarte is now Medicaid program director at the Guam Department of Public Health and Social Services.

One of the Fellows in the field of education is Daro Weital. He had had two years at the University of Hawaii, after which he began to teach school (he was paid by the hour—33 cents). He went on for another year at the Guam Territorial College, and then had a U.N. Fellowship to study rural schools in the Philippines and in Rangoon, Burma, in 1960–61. An Opportunity Fellowship allowed him to receive a B.S. degree in elementary education in the Philippines, and he returned to be supervisor of elementary education at home.

Several years later, under the Education Professional Development Act he went on to the University of Hawaii where he took a Master's degree in educational administration. He continued to study for a second Master's degree in secondary education and in June 1971 was appointed deputy director of the Community College of Micronesia.

The eighteen or twenty men now in education or government in the Islands who have been helped by Opportunity Fellowships are important in themselves and in the service they perform—but they are perhaps quite as important as a symbol of what is needed educationally to develop public and private life on the Islands.

How the need for education in the Islands can be more rapidly met than it is now,.is hard to say. Though there were few Trust Territory Opportunity Fellows, their experience testifies to one of the major problems Heine reported: "Whenever a teacher has acquired enough training to do a good job, the attractions from other jobs pull him away." At least five of the Fellows holding government posts started out as teachers, sought fellowship training to make them better teachers, and then turned from teaching to political life. Perhaps that is where they were needed most—and perhaps the original purpose they had and the training they received will prompt them to create a program for more adequate education for more people. Their influence in government might actually make them better able to achieve it.

Chapter 8

THE APPALACHIANS

Very poor white people abound in this country. The Appalachian Mountain region is a particularly depressed area—a place where there is not only great poverty and educational possibilities are very low, but also where the conditions that provide a living make it unlikely that most people born to the environment have normal leverage for bettering their condition.

Out of that environment came a small band of intellectuals whom the Foundation can feel proud to have supported. It is a *very* small band—only thirteen in all. There was not, for the "mountain white" group, the kind of recruitment effort that has been made for other deprived groups.

Berea College—itself one of the most important centers of concern about young people in Appalachia—has been a source of candidates. Four of the Opportunity Fellows were from Berea—three students and one faculty member. Most of the others had been educated in other southern colleges and universities.

Of the thirteen Fellows, nine took the advanced degrees for which the fellowship was granted. Four have been lost sight of. Among the nine, there are now four Ph.D.'s, one Ed.D., one M.S.W. and one M.A., one physician, and one lawyer. Most of these men and women came from rural areas in Georgia, Tennessee, Kentucky, and the Ozark Mountain region.

From William H. Baker one gets a classical picture of a young person's experience in a mountain coal-mining region:

My father was fired by the Pruden Coal Company of Tennessee for his activities in the coal strike of 1922 ... blacklisted by executives of the larger mining operations through the Southern Appalachian Region ... forcibly ejected from the community by hired strike breakers. Moving to the mining town of Middleboro, Kentucky, my father worked for small "wagon mines" ... Another move carried the family deeper into the hills of Kentucky.... My high school days began in Whitesburg, Kentucky, in the depth of the Depression.

Drafted (he then had a family of three children), he served in the Marines from 1944 to 1946. Entering the armed forces was the turning point of his life. Discharged in 1946, he enrolled, under the G.I. bill, in Lincoln Memorial University in Harrogate, Tennessee. He took a B.A. there, a Master's degree at the University of Tennessee in 1955, and was awarded an Opportunity Fellowship in 1957. This started him on the way to a Ph.D. in economics in 1963. He is now dean of the School of Business Administration at the University of Tennessee at Martin.

This is a fairly common picture. A professor, sponsor of a student, wrote: "He comes from a very poor background, from the mountain section of the state, and from people who had little to do with education or any ambition above the general scramble for making a living." And about another applicant: "It is difficult for me to understand how a person with such outstanding ability can emerge from the cultural background of his family's income group in this area."

William Burkett, from the southern part of the Appalachian Mountains, one of the Berea graduates, had an Opportunity Fellowship in 1967–68 for social work training. He is now executive director of the Cave Run Comprehensive Care Center, which offers mental health services including a drug abuse program to a five-county area in rural northeastern Kentucky. He was a delegate to the White House Conference on Aging. Indeed, with one exception all these men and women continue to work in the South.

George B. Daniel, who came from a small farm in Georgia,

was a teacher of French at Berea College, where the dean and president selected him as the faculty member who should study abroad. They sponsored him for a Fulbright Fellowship and he spent a year at the University of Paris. "He uses the French language perfectly, with no American traces in his pronunciation." He was awarded an Opportunity Fellowship to start work on his Ph.D. from the University of North Carolina, where he is now Alumni Distinguished Professor of Freshman Instruction and professor of French.

Mary Ray Johnson, from Kentucky, had an Opportunity Fellowship to begin her medical studies at the University of Louisville Medical School. She wrote:

> I have full confidence that I shall carry out this lifetime project completely. For me this will mean the culmination and continuation of my ambitions—the opportunity to serve the needy in the field that beckons me, in the place that I love, in the work that I like, and where I am needed very badly.

Dr. Johnson, now the mother of four sons, is chief of the Pediatric Department and chief of staff at the Williamson Appalachian Regional Hospital.

One of these nine Fellows is dean of students in Frostburg State College in Maryland; another is head of the department of animal sciences at the Virginia Polytechnic Institute and State University in Virginia. One is an attorney with a law firm in Charlotte, North Carolina; one was executive director of the YWCA in High Point, North Carolina, until she retired on the birth of her son; and the ninth, the only one to have left Appalachia, is a professor of zoology at the University of Michigan.

Chapter 9

DISPLACED PERSONS

The painful history of thousands of refugees who sought to re-establish their lives in this country needs no retelling. A small number among those thousands found their way to the John Hay Whitney Foundation and the Opportunity Fellowship Program to make places for themselves here.

One of the tragic and often repeated stories of the emigrés who poured into New York and San Francisco and Los Angeles from the 1930s to the 1950s is the sorry permanent adjustment many of them had to make to life on an entirely different intellectual, cultural, and social level than the life that was snatched from them. This is because they were untrained or what they were trained to do could not be done here; or they were perhaps even too advanced in a profession to start it anew here; or they were ill or too old; or perhaps the dislocations had been too great on all counts.

The twenty-two displaced men and women who received Opportunity Fellowships, most of them between 1955 and 1960, had had the same experiences as other victims of the war years. Many came from families who had been refugees twice or even three times. Among them was one from a Russian emigré family that fled to Estonia and fled again to Germany when Russia took over the Baltic states; a Latvian woman who spent seven years in a DP camp in Germany after the war; a Slovenian student who would have had a good chance for free studies if he had been willing to declare himself for the Nazis and whose family was later deprived of its property by the Russians and spent five years in a DP camp in Italy; Jewish refugees from Germany and Poland.

A family of intellectuals in Russia, dissatisfied with the Soviet public schools, had arranged tutorial studies for their daughter. She later attended Moscow University, left there in 1946 and came to the New School in New York. A Polish student who escaped when the Russians came in 1939, was caught in Hungary and sent to a concentration camp, escaped after three months and joined a Polish contingent in the French campaign of 1940. A Hungarian student was involved in the 1956 revolution; orders came to engage in no retaliatory activities, but to remain in the clinics and "protect our wounded from Russian annihilation." He stayed one week to transfer wounded. "By that time it was evident that the Russian military machine had completely crushed the revolt." He escaped across the Austrian border.

These are men and women who came to this country bent on continuing their education here. Most of them were fairly young—university age—and most had been students or, by the events of conquest and planned destruction, prevented from being students. Some of them had carried on their education under all sorts of abnormal conditions.

Frank Silbajoris, a Lithuanian wrote:

In 1942 when I was sixteen the Germans attacked the Soviet Union and occupied our country. Under both Russians and Germans I continued to go to school. Under the Russians the school system was changed, and Russian was introduced as the principal foreign language. The Germans made the German language obligatory, eliminating Russian. Under both systems we continued to be taught French and Latin.

In the fall of 1944 ... the retreating Germans took me and my brother to Southern Austria to work as laborers, delivering food supplies to the German army. During this period I spoke three languages constantly: Lithuanian and Russian, since my fellow workers were members of those nationalities, German with our superiors. At the end of the war I hitch-hiked from Austria to Augsberg, Germany, where I entered a D.P. camp being organized under American authority. The first thing I did was to complete my high school course; and made considerable progress in Latvian and Estonian, as well as advancing my ability to use Russian, German, and English.

In 1947 I was admitted to the University of Mainz and continued my studies until 1949, majoring in English language and literature, at the same time taking French literature.

In 1949 he received from the International Refugee Organization applications for scholarships to United States colleges; he filled some out and then he and his brother, without waiting for the results, came to the United States under the regular displaced persons quota. He was working at Schrafft's, planning to save money until he could afford to enter college, when he received a letter from Antioch College that had traveled to Germany and back; it offered him a scholarship, and he entered there the following fall.

The experiences of these displaced persons had been traumatic and their road was hard—but they were especially able individuals and the road was perhaps not so hard for them as for other refugees. Most of them made their way in this country to important eastern colleges—Harvard and Columbia, Swarthmore, Brandeis, Sarah Lawrence, and Radcliffe.

They were in this country for four or five years before they applied for Opportunity Fellowships—most of them taking undergraduate work—and fifteen of the twenty-two had already taken degrees in American colleges at the time they applied. Some had been on national scholarships and university scholarships as undergraduates, and won Woodrow Wilson and Fulbright Fellowships afterward. In most cases the Opportunity Fellowship started them off on graduate study. To some it gave a year off to complete a dissertation in a graduate program well on its way.

A few of these Opportunity Fellows had begun or were advanced in their professional work at home—two men who had been practicing law were also on the law faculties of their universities. In the United States these two used their Opportunity Fellowships to take law degrees, at Harvard and St.

Johns, and are practicing here. Three others in the group took medical degrees and one a dental degree. One went to MIT for engineering and one took a Master of Arts in Teaching, at Yale. Eleven followed their graduate studies through to the Ph.D.; the remaining three took no advanced degrees.

Most of these men and women—fifteen of the twenty-two —moved directly from graduate study into professional academic life. One, whose field was the history of medieval art, became curator of the great Robert Lehman collection. He had been a curator at home, and the confiscation of his library and of the manuscripts of books he had written, and the refusal of the authorities to give him transcripts of his career at the university where he had taken the Ph.D., are a tragic example of the particular sufferings of intellectuals in those years.

One physician is a psychiatrist in private practice, a second became an instructor and chief medical resident at the University of Minnesota Hospital, and the third is on the faculty of the Dartmouth Medical School. The dentist was in private practice and has retired.

Those who joined university faculties have taught at City College in New York, Brandeis, Wellesley, Georgia State, Hunter College, Fairleigh Dickinson, the University of Colorado, Ohio State, Harvard, George Washington University, Arizona State, and the University of Michigan. Their principal fields are Slavic and Germanic languages and literature, and political Science and history; there are a few psychologists and sociologists among them. Their level of achievement is high for they had not only ability but also commitment and the capacity to transcend extraordinary disruptions.

Chapter 10

FELLOWSHIPS
in the
ARTS

Earlier sections of this book describe changes in the character, motivations, and goals of fellowship applicants over the years. The program thus took on a character consistent with the original expectations of the Foundation but responding in its development to the winds of change in the world at large.

Other changes—in the administration of the program and the population it served—were the result both of the problems faced in making the selections and of questions of funding. The changes of this sort affected principally the arts.

In the beginning the purpose to serve the humanities seemed a clear mandate. The arts belong to the humanities, obviously, so applications from young artists—painters, dancers, musicians, and theater people—were to be considered along with others. No prior decision was made about how much of the available funds would go for academic study and how much for study of the arts. However, it soon became clear that a different set of criteria had to be developed for people in the arts than for those who planned graduate or professional study.

Other problems had to be dealt with: At what stage in an artist's life should he be eligible for an Opportunity Fellowship? Decisions about that were more difficult to make than decisions about college graduates who wanted to proceed to graduate study, even taking into account the maverick character of some of the academic applicants. An effort was made to award fellowships in the arts insofar as possible "at a time in a candidate's career which would make a substantial difference in his ability to move from a purely student category to that of beginning professional." Also it was decided to make no renewal awards in the arts; early in the program it was realized that awards in these fields could become endless in the process of a person's artistic development.

The difficulties in making policy for awards in the arts are recorded in a report written after the program had been in existence for ten years:

There are many levels of artistic development which are difficult to define. There is an indeterminate period of basic training. This period of study may be formal or self-taught, or a combination of both. Awards have not been given to candidates in this stage of development largely because they do not measure up competitively with others who apply, and the juries can scarcely ascertain what their possibilities are. Many potential candidates from the groups in most pressing need of more education conceivably fall into this category. But whereas the badly or inadequately trained candidate in biology or English may be favorably considered by the program, his counterpart in the Arts is not likely to be (and usually does not apply).

At a second general stage a candidate is ready for specialized training of the best sort. This may mean time to paint and study aspects of our great art tradition, or a trip to Europe, or a concentrated period of writing. This is the stage which has been given most attention by the Foundation, but it tends to spill over into the third state:

A number of our Fellows have already been to Europe, had Fulbrights, sung in Town Hall, published short works, or had exhibits in group or even one-man shows.

The last paragraph describes the artist who is already on the long road of his professional development, and the Foundation came to feel that it had no measurable design for determining how much to invest in him and for how long. It is the most expensive period of training, and achieving professional status needs not only continued training but also, especially in the performing arts, all the expensive corollaries—wardrobe, professional management, publicity—that help create a public.

When the jury had struggled with these problems for ten years, it was decided to separate the program of academic awards and the program for awards in the arts, and for the next five years there were separate juries for each of the arts, who gave auditions or reviewed the work of painters and sculptors.

At the end of that five-year period, the Foundation decided to eliminate fellowships in the visual and performing arts and limit the program to applicants for academic study. The problems presented by short-term support for artists and the difficulty of making judgments about them were not the only reasons. In addition, changes in the Internal Revenue Code and Regulations made it difficult to carry on the plans originally envisioned by the Foundation and led to a decrease in the funds available for fellowships. Moreover, at this point, increased federal appropriations for the arts supported the work of artists on a scale that could not be remotely reached by the Foundation.

So the following account of the Opportunity Fellowships in the performing and visual arts covers the period from the inception of the program in 1950 to 1965, after which no art fellowships were granted.

WHO THEY WERE

During the fifteen years it existed, the arts program awarded eighty-six fellowships in music, dance and theater; all but ten of the recipients were black. It awarded seventy-five in painting, sculpture, and other visual arts, thirty-nine to blacks and 36 to others—twenty-four of them to Chinese or Japanese Americans. That is, the number of awards to the non-black minority groups (and the number of applicants for such awards) was always very small. Of the Orientals, nearly half came from Hawaii.

The account of musicians that follows speaks mainly of the black musicians—there were so few others. It is not an evaluation of their "success" so much as it is a kind of profile of their experience as they follow, most of them with relentless conviction, the difficult road of development in the arts. For the musician there must be a continuing audience, and the record of this group of young artists is a poignant account of the enormous effort to achieve the audience, as well as continuous and intensive study.

I have mentioned in another connection the usefulness of an Opportunity Fellowship in making a student more visible in his profession and in his search for other fellowship support. This is strikingly true in the case of the Fellows in music. This advantage is in addition to the relief from the need to earn while studying. The students in the arts who have won Opportunity Fellowships have the same history as other students of readiness to work at anything—physical labor, household service, office jobs; as librarians, teachers, postal clerks—until they can find support. They have far less chance, as we know, to support themselves by professional work when they have completed their studies than young people in other fields.

Of the seventy-six awards to blacks in the performing arts, about sixty were in music, the others in dance or theater. And of the music awards more than forty were for the study of singing. There were a few piano awards, a few for music composition, a few for musicology or ethnic music, and, in the later years of the fellowships, some for the study of percussion instruments. The awards were more varied later on.

THE FELLOWSHIPS

SINGERS

The singers illustrate well the pattern of life of talented young persons seeking a place in the world of the arts, because all these students had talent, good voices, and high motivation for study. And it is a gratifying demonstration that the "Opportunity Fellowships" lived up to their name in two ways: in the opportunities the recipients had for creative musical life in the years of study under the fellowship, and in the access it gave them to later grants awarded by other foundations or institutions.

The list of awards won by this group of singers is impressive. All of them hoped to have public careers, and about fifteen expected from the beginning to teach. Also, it is interesting to follow the history of both groups in terms of the financial aid they were able to get and of their lives as public performers.

In all but four cases of the students seeking careers as singers, awards after the Opportunity Fellowship helped them to continue their studies. Out of a group of twenty-five, intent on the opera and concert stage as a lifework, twenty won Marian Anderson awards or Martha Baird Rockefeller awards, or both, and a broad scattering of other awards, from the Metropolitan Opera, private music foundations, and other sources. Four later won Fulbright awards.

Fellowship aid for the arts had never been organized as was aid for science or even study in the humanities; it had always been sporadic, short-term, and undependable. These students lived precarious financial lives. Moreover, Europe as the place to study was important for most of them by the time the Opportunity Fellowship came along, and residence there prohibited them from earning money as graduate students in our universities can do, and as the Opportunity Fellows, particularly, were so accustomed to do.

Their reports also bring out the professional opportunities they found during their fellowship year, which was likely to bring a large and enviable experience of travel, study, and singing. To be sure, for those at an early stage of their training the grant was for continued study at Juilliard, the Eastman School, or some other American institution. But those who received fellowships when they were a little farther along —whatever the final outcome of the effort to become an opera or concert singer—took off for Europe; and they had opportunities to perform in various European countries and elsewhere.

As these Fellows continue their study, and emerge as developed singers, the reports of performances multiply. The Scandinavian countries, particularly Sweden, sought them out and a number of them sang either in concert or opera in Stockholm. They toured in North Africa, South America, and the Far East; sang at Bayreuth, with the Berlin orchestra, in Vienna, Israel, and Switzerland. One Fellow followed a series of appearances abroad by a trip home where she sang in Atlanta at the first concert with an integrated audience; others sang for a number of years with Radio Free Europe.

The strong impression one gets is of an almost breathlessly intensive effort to keep before the public which singers must have; that in many cases the opportunity to be heard seemed greater in Europe than in the United States. The difficulties and opportunities are illustrated in the following ten-year history of an Opportunity Fellow now teaching in the New York schools, following on his fellowship of 1959–60.

I returned to America in March of this year [1970] after trying for ten years to forge an operatic career in Germany.

I left the country in 1960 . . . to work and study at the famed Festspielhaus in Bayreuth. From Bayreuth I took up residence in Berlin, and sang for two years throughout East Germany as a Lieder singer. Later I was engaged as leading bass with the Israel National Opera. I sang there two seasons. Finally I returned to Germany to resume my career there. After many auditions I received a guest contract with the Hamburg Staatsoper, and sang with great success the world premiere of Gunther Schuller's much acclaimed opera *The Visitation*. In 1967 I came to New York with the Hamburg Opera and sang the American premiere of *The Visitation* at the Metropolitan Opera.

Last season I was engaged at the Volksoper in Vienna for 12 performances of George Gershwin's *Porgy and Bess*. At the close of my engagement in Vienna, I flew to New York to sing in a recital in Brooklyn. While in America I went to the Board of Education to inquire if my teaching license was still valid. They told me it was, and I returned to the country for good in March.

Since then I went back to Europe in April to sing the French premiere of *The Visitation*. I was invited to Earlham College last month to sing a performance of the Beethoven IX Symphony. On the 18th of December

I will return to Berlin to sing a series of concerts with the Berlin Symphony.

In conclusion, I feel I am doing better financially and artistically since I returned to New York. It is very difficult for a black man, no matter how talented, to make a career as an opera singer; and the demand for Lieder singers is not that great.

Another Opportunity Fellow used the fellowship, granted in 1958, for a year of study abroad. After a year she returned, earned her living by clerking in stores and working in playgrounds and community centers. A few years later she was engaged for a series of concerts in this country, and then returned to Europe. She has never returned to the United States.

Some former Fellows have continued to carry on their careers abroad, whether occasionally, between engagements, or by taking time off from continuing employment in this country, or else making their main base abroad. Mattawilda Dobbs illustrates on a distinguished level the kind of European-based career some of the Opportunity Fellows have been able to follow, after that year of mobility the fellowship gave them. Now in the midst of a fine career as an opera and concert singer, Miss Dobbs writes:

Winning the John Hay Whitney Opportunity Fellowship meant a great deal to me, coming just at the crucial period in which I was to decide whether or not I would be able to make a career as a singer. I had completed my basic vocal and musical studies and needed something to give me an impetus, i.e. the opportunity to travel to Europe, study leisurely, and explore the possibilities of starting a career in Europe. This is precisely what the Fellowship gave me, and since I was successful in launching a career in singing during the two years I was living on my grant, I am immensely grateful for having been given the opportunity.

After graduating from Spelman College, Miss Dobbs began four years of musical study in New York. During those years she also studied Spanish at Columbia University and took a

Master's degree. One summer of that time she spent at the University of Mexico and sang in the university's Festival of Music. She won scholarships that enabled her to study in the Opera Workshop of the Mannes Music School and the Opera Workshop of the Berkshire Music Center at Tanglewood. As she writes, it was the Opportunity Fellowship that freed her to study in Paris for two years, to work on a Spanish repertoire in Spain, and to win first prize at the international music competition of the Conservatory of Music at Geneva. In the seasons that followed she sang concerts in the Scandinavian capitals, in Belgium, Holland, France, Italy, and England, and made her opera debut at La Scala in Milan. In 1954 she returned to this country, but only briefly, and in the years since she has a long history of opera and concert performances in this country, in Mexico and Central America, in Australia, in the Soviet Union, and all over Europe. Since 1957 she has made her home in Stockholm and sings frequently in the Royal Swedish Opera, but she continues to sing with major opera companies throughout the world. She makes an annual concert tour in the United States, and sings with the Metropolitan.

Other musicians have made their careers abroad—Rhea Jackson, living in Germany, sings with the opera in Sweden and Norway, with orchestras in Belgium, Holland, Germany, and Yugoslavia. Debria Brown, also living in Germany, having established herself in Europe, thinks of coming back to create a career here.

In view of the heartbreaking obstacles to the kind of musical career these young artists envisioned for themselves, it is moving to discover how many of them have persisted. Some have abandoned their careers; one Fellow of the middle 1950s studied abroad for two years after receiving the fellowship, but seems to have had no musical career. He has worked in Harlem youth agencies and community centers and with the Peace Corps; he is now a deputy director of a community-action training institute.

Another singer writes from a farm in upstate New York where he is living with his wife and five children "trying to revive a run-down old fruit farm":

My wife and I are writing a method for parents to teach their children to read and write at home before sending them to school, designed for children of non-white parents. It will be published in the Spring of 1971.... I also intend to spend some time working with the early childhood materials development section of the Congress of African Peoples. And, if we live and the world lasts long enough, we intend to design an alternative system of education that goes from shortly after birth through puberty.

I've quit singing entirely. Although we have, personally, much to sing about, Nixon, the SST, Agnew, Buckley, the CIA, U.S. Navy, the local police department and other such incredible fixtures in the American scene weigh most heavily in the negative direction. Some day, God willing, we shall.

Some singers have established themselves in music schools or music departments of universities or public schools; some of them also appear frequently in concert and opera in this country. For some of these it was a matter of deciding to settle for the second best—the road to a purely public career in music was too hard or too long. However, more of them had planned a teaching career from the beginning. One application said: "I want to study the music of Africa and India, and I want to teach." Another: "I want the skill and the chance to sing; and I want to make music an important part of the lives of young people." Today they sing with local opera companies, give concerts, direct choirs and choruses, and participate in music festivals.

In the field of music, several applicants carried on graduate study under fellowships and are having interesting academic and musical careers: One of them produced a number of albums of Negro folk songs, wrote on Negro folk music, taught music, and served as chairman of a college music department. Another is an ethnomusicologist who is working on the music of African countries.

A final thought: In other places in this book I have written of the particular problems faced by people of minority races in carrying on their professional lives. The prejudices, the economic problems, the obstacles to fair competition for recognition and place that exist in other fields exist in the arts as well, although (sometimes for the wrong reasons) black artists have had a kind of welcome into the society that black professionals in other fields have not.

But as one reads the history of these able young people, in their effort to become accomplished and to become recognized, a circumstance peculiar to *their* vocation impresses itself on one. And one wonders when, if ever, skin color will no longer determine what parts in the opera a singer is permitted to sing. One wonders, of course, reading the post-fellowship history of political scientists, historians, and sociologists, how many of them chose to teach in segregated colleges after their studies were completed in the 1950s or early 1960s—how many of them found no other places to teach. (*Their* situation has improved a little since 1965!)

With the singers the recurrent listing of *Porgy and Bess, Aida, Four Saints in Three Acts* as operas in which these talented people performed underlines the destructively limited chance they have had for the kind of development that should have been open to them all. For a few the list of parts sung is quite wide, but not for many. Studying in Paris in 1952 on her fellowship, one musician sang in *Porgy and Bess* in Paris the next year and then went on tour in Europe in the musical. In 1960 she was still on tour, this time in South America, in the same musical. There is no record of her having sung any other role.

OTHER MUSICIANS

Nine awards were made to pianists. One had a subsequent Fulbright award and spent the year studying in Belgium, and two early Fellows had concert careers abroad. Each of these went into college teaching. One of the last Fellows in music is now in the Doctor of Musical Arts program at Juilliard and is a church organist; one participated in the Third International Competition in Moscow, and is a professional accompanist. Two of the nine awards went to Japanese Americans, one of whom was to study at the Juilliard School and one in Paris; the first joined the faculty of Youngstown University after concerts in New York and San Francisco, the second won a Rockefeller Fellowship a year after the Opportunity Fellowship, remained in Paris, and played concerts in London and Paris. She returned home to head the music department of Abbott Academy, and subsequently to teach privately.

Six fellowships went to students of music composition, and, like the piano students, most of them have supported themselves by teaching—one at a 600 school in New York and also at Hunter, and he makes jazz recordings. One is a music professor at Rutgers. One became, after the fellowship, chairman of the Fine Arts Division of Central State College, in Ohio, another is executive director of the Inner City Cultural Center in Los Angeles, and another, also continuing to compose, is the program associate in the humanities of the Institute for Service to Education. The only Mexican American to be awarded a fellowship for composition won third prize in the Queen Elizabeth of Belgium chamber music contest.

PAINTERS AND SCULPTORS

Fellowships in the visual arts were divided mainly between blacks and Orientals. Of the sixty-nine fellowships, thirty-nine went to blacks, twenty-four to Japanese Americans and Chinese Americans, and only six to others. (Applications from Mexican Americans, Puerto Ricans, and Indians were very rare.) Of those six fellowships, three were in painting and sculpture, the other three in photography and ceramics.

It is, if anything, more difficult to make pronouncements about the success of painters or their contributions to art, than about the success of musicians. Concert and opera engagements may measure the public success of a musician, or one-man shows measure that of a painter, but we all know that any responsible judgment about either as artists cannot be made on such grounds.

As with the musicians, perhaps the best we can do is to give the image of their lives as artists that the record reveals.

Of the thirty-nine fellowships awarded to black applicants in the visual arts, twenty-eight were for painting or sculpture, the rest for photography, history of art, scenic design, and museum study.

Twelve of the painters or sculptors on whom we have recent information have exhibited or are now represented in permanent collections of major museums in this country and abroad. Eight others have had exhibitions in public museums. There appear to be only three who have given up painting as a major part of their lives.

Ten of these artists, most of them men and women who have also exhibited widely, are teaching in universities—Queens College, Boston University, Howard University, Temple University, the New School for Social Research, and other places. Some are teaching at art institutes, some of them have been artists in residence at colleges around the country, and a few are in the public school systems.

Both men who had fellowships to study the history of art taught later at universities, and the one who studied to be a curator, and who had had two years of study in London before the Opportunity Fellowship and a Fulbright after it, has served at several universities as teacher and curator.

The painters who had Opportunity Fellowships in the 1950s have by now an unusual record of later awards, exhibitions, and purchases by public museums. Richard Mayhew went on to the MacDowell Colony a year after his grant, and this was followed by an American Academy grant, a Merrill Foundation grant, and a Tiffany Foundation award. He has exhibited at the Chicago Art Institute, the Carnegie Museum International Exhibit, the Whitney Museum, and many other museums and galleries.

Charles W. White held a Julius Rosenwald Fellowship before his Opportunity Fellowship, and many awards, gold medals, and citations after it, and his exhibitions are worldwide. His drawings have often been reproduced in works on art, and several volumes of them have been published.

Walter Williams studied in France, Denmark, and Sweden on his Opportunity Fellowship and has spent much of his life abroad since then, either in Mexico or in Europe. In 1964 he participated in an exhibition in Copenhagen of American black artists living and working abroad. Five of the ten painters in that exhibition were Opportunity Fellows. It was organized to raise funds for civil rights causes in the United States. Mr. Williams was artist in residence at Fisk University in 1968–69.

Benny Andrews had taught at the New School for Social Research, and was visiting artist at the California State College at Hayward. He is now on the faculty of Queens College in New York. He has exhibited at major museums and galleries throughout the United States and is included in many major collections. After the Opportunity Fellowships he was awarded the Dorne Fellowship at Bridgeport University, and was a grantee of the New York State Council on the Arts for 1971. He is much involved in issues relating to black artists and their art and has written on these subjects for the *New York Times* and for art journals.

Sam Middleton has had a worldwide career and has worked in a great variety of media. For ten years he has made his home in the Netherlands, and before that he had one-man exhibitions of his paintings in a dozen countries. He has produced lithographs and has also designed for ballet, avant-garde theater, and musicals. His work has been featured in the showrooms of an international maker of fine furniture, and in the past year he had another month-long one-man show in Holland. He taught for three years at the Netherlands Royal Academy in 's Hertogenbosch.

Barbara Chase Riboud is also working abroad, in Paris. The year after her fellowship in 1958 she appeared in the Carnegie Museum International Exhibit in Pittsburgh, has exhibited in Paris, Rome, Spoleto, and Dakar, but has also maintained her connections with this country. She exhibited in the Whitney Sculpture Annual in 1970, had one-man shows the same year in Boston and New York, and will have another in New York in 1972.

Paul Keene, who had a two-year Opportunity Fellowship, had studied in Paris before his fellowship and spent the first fellowship year painting in the Caribbean. He has exhibited in Paris, Genoa, Haiti, and Nigeria as well as in the United States.

Of the painters, Paul Keene, William Majors, Benny Andrews, John Wilson, Charles White, and Richard Mayhew have also been teaching.

About the same number of black artists are spending full time at their work; several have been engaged in jobs related to art—one owned a gallery, another went into advertising designing. Five we have lost sight of.

Of the ninety-six Orientals who won Opportunity Fellowships, thirty-two were in the arts—twenty-four painters and sculptors, eight writers, dancers, and musicians. This constitutes the largest proportion of fellowships in the arts awarded to any group, although the number to blacks was about the same.

Many of the Chinese and Japanese painters wanted to use the fellowship to work in New York. Like the singers for whom the fellowship provided the beginning of the kind of aid artists must have, a good many painters obtained other grants later.

J. C. Leong had taken Bachelor's and Master's degrees at the California College of Arts and Crafts. The year after his Opportunity Fellowship he had a number of one-man shows in New York and Los Angeles. Two years later he won a Fulbright award and painted and exhibited in Oslo and Copenhagen; the same paintings were later exhibited in New York. The next year he was awarded a Guggenheim grant to study in Italy. This was in 1960. He remained a number of years in Italy and exhibited very widely all through the 1960s in San Francisco, New York, and Rome.

George J. Myasaki, also from the California College of Arts and Crafts, intended from the first to go into teaching. He won a good many prizes, especially for his prints, was awarded a Guggenheim five years after his Opportunity Fellowship, and is now working in his studio and following the academic career he planned, on the faculty of the Art Department at the Berkeley campus of the University of California.

Frank S. Okada, one of the artists who wanted the Opportunity Fellowship for study in New York, came from the Cranbrook Academy of Art in Detroit. He studied in New York with the particular painter he had come to work with, and won a Fulbright to Japan the following year. Five years later a Guggenheim Fellowship gave him a year in Paris. He is now at the School of Architecture and Allied Arts of the University of Oregon; he has exhibited, mainly in the West, but also in Paris during his Guggenheim year.

About half the Oriental Americans who had fellowships in the visual arts came originally from Hawaii. Bob Ochikubo, another artist who wanted to work in New York, won a Guggenheim the year after his Opportunity Fellowship, to permit him to continue working in New York. For the thirteen years that have followed he has lived and worked there.

Shinkichi Tajiri, a sculptor who came originally from the Art Institute in Chicago, had studied in Europe for ten years before the Opportunity Fellowship and had a one-man show in Holland the year of the fellowship. He did a monumental sculpture on commission in Holland; two years after his fellowship he traveled to Japan, where he had an exhibition of his sculptures, and then returned to Holland. He has been a visiting professor at the Minneapolis School of Art, and has had shows in New York but makes his home and does his work abroad. He is now professor of sculpture at the Hochschule für Bildende Kunst in West Berlin. He was awarded the Grand Prix for a film at the First International Festival for Pornographic Films at Amsterdam, in 1970. He is now working on video projects for European museums.

Two Indians had Opportunity Fellowships in the visual arts. Fritz Scholder is an important artist and an important force in the Southwest, his work growing out of his interest in Indian life. A major exhibition of his work on the American Indian will be shown in 1972 at the National Fine Art Collection of the Smithsonian Institution in Washington, and in Europe.

As with other artists, many of the painters and sculptors (including some of the most successful) teach as they continue to paint. Ten of the twenty-eight black Opportunity Fellows in painting and sculpture went into teaching—at Michigan State, Manhattan Community College, Boston University, Queens College, and other institutions here and abroad. About the same number of black artists are spending full time at their painting. Several have been engaged in jobs related to art.

WRITERS

Twenty-six fellowships were awarded in creative writing, twenty of them to black writers. Typically, singers used their fellowships to take them to Europe, and painters used their fellowships to bring them to New York. A particular place to work was not so important for the writers—they wanted time:

> The reason I can think to claim, now, that time is all I need to pull together a solid first book of verse is that I feel I have gotten finally to that point where my own poetic voice is beginning to burgeon more clearly; and I need only a little time to hear it out. . . .
>
> A man writes as he does, and when he's ready, publishes books of his writings. Some kind of objective for me would be merely to work out a "space" to do all that in. This request for time is part of it.

This was the request of LeRoi Jones, now Imamu Amiri Baraka. He was by that time an experienced writer of verse and prose, published in avant-garde magazines and in anthologies. In the ten years after the Opportunity Fellowship he has become an important voice and one of the most important figures in the world of literature and action involving the lives of black people.

Scott Momaday, another writer who has become an increasingly important literary figure, and also an increasingly important spokesman for the Indian people, was awarded a fellowship to complete his doctoral dissertation at Stanford. He was born in Oklahoma and spent his early years on a New Mexico reservation, the son of parents who were teachers in the reservation school. He was graduated from the University of New Mexico and taught for a year in an Indian school on the Jicarilla Apache Reservation. To work with these young people he had to learn their language. He went on to graduate work at Stanford, where with the Opportunity Fellowship he was able to complete his degree, and he worked at the same time with Ivor Winters the writer. Writing and teaching have gone on together since then; he won a Guggenheim award, a few years after his Opportunity Fellowship, that again gave him time to write, and in 1969 he won the Pulitzer Prize for his novel *The House of Dawn*. He continues to write, to be active in Indian affairs, and to teach comparative literature at the University of California in Berkeley.

The writers have had varied writing and working lives; four of them published novels within a year or two after the Opportunity Fellowship, five of them have had plays produced, mainly off Broadway. The list of publications by Fellows also shows that about half of them have published poetry, and their short stories and poetry have found place in many anthologies.

Richard Gibson spent his fellowship year at the American Academy in Rome. George Houston Bass and Frank Brown took Master's degrees in the fellowship year and Carl Holman took a Master of Fine Arts at Yale, after which he taught at Clark College and published plays, poems, and reviews in the years that followed. Lonne Elder has lectured on playwriting at Brandeis, and taught and directed in workshops, as well as appearing in Broadway and off-Broadway productions. Margaret Danner, whose work was early published by *Poetry* magazine, became the assistant editor of that magazine and was poet in residence at Wayne University. These are the patterns most of the writing careers have followed.

Perhaps the most prolific of all is Benjamin Johnson, translator and critic of Italian literature. Johnson was one of the early Opportunity Fellows, and in the years that followed he has published hundreds of translations—short stories, poetry, novels, and essays on Italy, principally on the arts. He has translated Calvino, Pavese, Pratolini, and mainly, perhaps, Italo Svevo.

The black authors have sought and earned their literary

reputation as writers, not as black writers, but almost all of them have been closely involved with the lives and concerns of black people. Perhaps Benjamin Johnson, whose roots have been put down deep in the literature of Italy, has moved farther from a central concern with the lives of black people than any other.

ART EDUCATION

There were nine fellowships for the study of education in the arts or musicology. Eight went to black students and one to a Mexican American. Six of the nine Fellows subsequently held academic posts—at St. Augustine College, at Howard, at Bennett College in Greensboro, at Clark College, at Morgan State. The Mexican American in art education studied at New Mexico Highlands University on his Opportunity Fellowship in 1967–68 and the following year at the Brooklyn Museum Art School on a scholarship. In 1971 one Fellow was a professional harpist and was still studying. One has been lost sight of.

THE PERFORMING ARTS

Ten theater fellowships—six for producing and directing, four for acting—were granted, and eight in dance. In addition one fellowship was awarded for advanced academic study of theater.

Theater. Six of the theater Fellows are engaged in freelance producing, directing, or designing, and working with theater groups in colleges or elsewhere.

Edward Burbridge designs productions for Broadway, the Los Angeles Music Center, and the New York Metropolitan Opera Studio and is the resident designer for the Negro Ensemble Company in New York. He spent his Opportunity Fellowship year abroad and, he says, "the knowledge gained during my time at twelve European repertory theatres continues to provide stimulation and direction in my present work."

Luther James, who had been directing plays off Broadway and in stock when he received an Opportunity Fellowship, has most recently produced a TV series *On Being Black* for National Educational Television, and is now writer and director of television productions. He has taught at the Negro Ensemble Company and in his own studios in New York and Los Angeles.

Woodie King heads the *Arts for Living* program in New York, and is a contributing editor for *Black Theatre Magazine.* His fellowship allowed him, he says, "to work with some of the most famous theatrical administrators in New York as well as producers and directors—Lloyd Richards, Ossie Davis, LeRoi Jones, Ed Bullins; The Chelsea Theatre Center, American Place Theatre, and now the Henry Street Settlement, of which I have built the New Federal Theatre Project." He has had wide experience producing the work of writers of the black theater, and in directing plays both in and out of this theater. He is a writer of short stories, dramatic criticism, and feature articles and is the cultural arts director of Mobilization for Youth and a consultant on the arts and humanities of the Rockefeller Foundation.

George Houston Bass is director of Rites and Reason, the black theater at Brown University. Electa Twyman, the year after her fellowship, joined the theater faculty of Spelman College.

Two of the acting Fellows have left the theater, but the other two are still working at the problem of being an actor in New York.

Esther Jackson, who had an Opportunity Fellowship for a Ph.D. in drama—her interest was in a synthesis of music, dance, and drama for college and community theater—went on to teach drama at Adelphi College.

Dance. One Mexican American student received an Opportunity Fellowship for work in dance therapy and is now on the faculty of the Mannes School of Music. A Cherokee Indian girl, awarded a fellowship for dance, almost immediately on her arrival in New York was given the lead in the national company of *Irma la Douce,* and her career was on its way.

The fellowships led the other dance Fellows—the rest of them Black—into varied careers: Walter Nicks, ten years after his fellowship, to choreography and teaching in Stockholm; Beverlee Patton to work with folklore groups in the West Indies; Pearl Reynolds to a concert in Sweden. James F. Truitte is a faculty member in the Dance Division of the Conservatory of Music at the University of Cincinnati, the Dance Theatre of Harlem, and the YWCA Clark Center for the Performing Arts. Eleo Pomare taught and choreographed ballets for the Netherlands Dance Theatre and joined two other Opportunity Fellows in an electronic music project in the Netherlands for which Tajiri did a sculpture, Sam Middleton the paintings, and Pomare the dances. Pomare came back to organize his own dance company in New York.

Chapter 11

ENDING THE FELLOWSHIPS: BEGINNING A NEW PLAN

The last of the Opportunity Fellowships were awarded for the year 1971–72, and the program ended; but the minorities for whom these fellowships were created are still among the most deprived in this country and continue to suffer the hazards of an increasingly tumultuous world in the most extreme way.

In 1950, Opportunity Fellowships were established to help individuals among them surmount the barriers to full opportunity all of them faced. Changes have taken place since then—the sharpest, most violent, and maybe the most productive have come about in the past five years. The attitudes, expectations, and demands of the most repressed parts of American society have shifted, become visible and vocal; and it has become clear that, while the need for opportunities to surmount the barriers they face remains, the need to attack the barriers has become inescapable.

At no time in the history of this country have the dislocations in the lives of black people, Mexican Americans, Puerto Ricans, American Indians and other disfranchised poor been the kind of front-page news they are now—the cause of legislation, protest, and turmoil in the education, economic life, and lives of ordinary citizens. We now know responsibility cannot be escaped.

Assistance such as the Opportunity Fellowships provided is still greatly needed, and as the story of the John Hay Whitney Fellowships ends, one sees belated efforts by universities, government, and private industry to provide it. The effort of the Ford Foundation programs, undertaken in 1971, to serve colleges where thousands of black students are being educated and to provide massive financial help to such students, will take another step toward dealing with the dislocations. But it is clear that only by bringing about basic change in economic, political, educational, and other social institutions can there be basic change in the conditions of life of disfranchised people.

The John Hay Whitney Foundation has decided, after twenty-five years and its service to nearly a thousand Opportunity Fellows, to use its funds toward such change. The new programs of the Foundation, initiated in 1971, will direct its efforts toward making educational and governmental agencies more responsive to the needs of that part of our population. Many men and women who have held Opportunity Fellowships are now engaged in such activities. They and others will help to identify persons and circumstances which, with Foundation support, might serve these purposes.

Part Two

THE
WHITNEY-FULBRIGHT
PROFESSORS

Chapter 12

THE
WHITNEY-FULBRIGHT
PROFESSORS

In 1951, during the same period of innovation in which the John Hay Whitney Foundation created the John Hay Fellows Program and the Opportunity Fellowship Program, it created also a series of professorships that sent to colleges around the country visiting professors from all parts of the globe. In 1954 it pioneered conferences to orient foreign professors to the American educational scene.

These were the years in which blocked American funds abroad were being used, under the Fulbright Act of 1946, to pay travel expenses for teachers and research scholars sought by American universities. Under the American side of the Fulbright Act, a university appointed a foreign professor for a year and paid his salary; his travel expenses were paid out of the government funds. To aid this program the Committee for the International Exchange of Persons (CIEP), an offshoot of the Conference Board of Associated Research Councils, was set up in Washington. A series of binational commissions screened applicants abroad and sent appropriate names to the committee. Universities here made their wants known, and appointments were made through the agency of the committee.

The interest of the Foundation had been established—it was engaged in supporting education in the humanities; it was interested in giving able young people the opportunity to work with established scholars. Its Opportunity Fellowships served principally college graduates headed for further study; its John Hay Fellowships served high school teachers and, through them, high school students. The new project was to serve foreign professors and, through them, American college undergraduates. The Visiting Professors project, to be established the next year, would serve the same general purpose.

FOREIGN PROFESSORS FOR DISADVANTAGED COLLEGES

Dr. Charles Johnson, who as consultant to the Foundation had been instrumental in developing the Foundation programs—indeed he had made some of the imaginative suggestions that gave it direction—pointed out to the Foundation that twice as many Fulbright professors who were coming here were in the natural sciences as were in the social sciences and the humanities. Moreover, most of them were here to do research and to teach graduate students. He suggested that the Foundation support a small group of foreign scholars who would come here primarily to teach undergraduates.

It was also true that a disproportionate number of the foreign scholars went to the academic centers of the country, to the large universities and to the prosperous colleges that could afford to make such appointments. The year before the Whitney–Fulbright program was set up, 278 foreign scholars came to this country on Fulbright travel grants; only seven of them went to the South and none to any Rocky Mountain state or to the Northwest.

SELECTING THE COLLEGES

The new program was instituted in March 1951, to begin the following fall, with four annual professorships. The CIEP furnished the Foundation with a list of colleges that might be interested. The Whitney–Fulbright professors were engaged to teach in colleges that could not otherwise have afforded the appointments, many of them in the South and West. The colleges were asked to describe the field in which they hoped to have a visiting professor teach, and whether they favored some particular nationality.

The response of the list of possible host colleges, selected by the CIEP to participate, is interesting—fewer than half expressed interest; a few sent negative replies; the others did not reply at all. According to the records of the CIEP, seventy-five additional inquiries were sent to Midwest colleges which were not in urban centers; about the same percentage of replies was received. To help the CIEP decide among the applicants, the Humanities Committee of the Foundation asked the colleges to send full accounts of how they wanted to use the visitor, what he would teach, how his teaching would fit the program of the college, what kind of living arrangements he would have, and how the college would like him to take part in the life of the campus and the community. It was the view of the Foundation that both visitors and institutions should make the widest use of their time on a college campus —that this should be an opportunity for the professor and his family to experience life in the new environment as fully as they could. These professors were not to fill vacancies but to add to the curriculum. They were not to have more than six hours weekly of classroom teaching, since they were also to have an opportunity to participate in the life of the college and the community. Colleges were asked to indicate whether the visitor might be shared with other colleges nearby.

Each professor was to be appointed to two institutions during the year—preferably in different sections of the country—one semester in each. This device would acquaint the professor with more of the country and would allow more institutions to participate.

SELECTING THE PROFESSORS

The binational selection committee for each country in the Fulbright Program was now asked to nominate two possible candidates each year for the Whitney–Fulbright appointments in the humanities and social sciences.

This program was not calculated to attract internationally known research scholars from abroad who wanted the prestige of association with an internationally known American institution. The prospect had to be attractive to people who would like the life of an undergraduate college, who wanted to teach undergraduate students, and who were interested in this way of coming to know something about the United States. A number of established scholars did apply for these professorships, but many of the candidates were able younger men and women, interested in expanding their intellectual, academic, and personal lives by association with American students and the American people. They came from far parts of the world to colleges of which they knew little or nothing. Looking back they many times emphasized—even more than the Foundation did—how important it was to discover that, educationally, Boston, New Haven, and New York are not all of the United States.

The CIEP, out of its experience with the Fulbright Exchange Program, selected a panel of foreign teacher applicants appropriate to the colleges applying for them. The list of professors was reviewed by the Humanities Committee of the Foundation.

AMERICAN EDUCATION A "FOREIGN COUNTRY"

Circumstances have changed greatly since 1951—the stream of students and faculty crossing the Atlantic and the Pacific to study and teach has in the intervening twenty years reached dimensions unimaginable at that time. But even now American students and teachers, and foreign students and teachers, do not understand each other's educational system very well and find they have to take time to learn. In the 1950s the lack of knowledge and understanding was enormous. Each professor knew he had been selected because the host institution wanted someone in his field and because his record was of interest. But teaching comfortably in an American college, or the undergraduate part of a university, presented problems that the newcomer did not know existed, and that the Americans did not know were problems.

Reports of the difficulties that Whitney–Fulbright professors (and other foreign professors) faced in teaching American undergraduates soon came back to the Foundation and the CIEP. At the Foundation, the wish of the Humanities Committee, the Foundation staff, and the Foundation trustees themselves that the program should be made as useful as possible led to the decision to try to give the arriving professors a better understanding of what they would meet here—

and to give American professors who would be working with them a better understanding not only of what the visitors brought with them but also what they needed to know.

The visitors, whatever their countries, came out of a university environment by comparison with which our academic life, by its extent and variety alone, appeared unusual and sometimes fantastic. Often, at least in 1950, even the most sophisticated of them had little conception of the enormous range of our educational institutions. It is a broad range even when only liberal arts institutions are considered—state universities, great private colleges and universities, small private colleges for men or women or for both, plus the municipal colleges and community and junior colleges. The roster is long enough for us who live with this great variety—it is both long and confusing for those who do not. The absence of a central educational authority, and the consequent absence of common academic standards, was a cause for surprise and sometimes dismay. The central place of the undergraduate college in our educational system and our national life often astounded the visitor, as did the range of the curriculum and the diversity of purposes it serves, and the wide variation in ability and knowledge among American undergraduates.

Not only the design of higher education in this country, but also scores of practical matters have often confused the visitor and delayed, until he could cope with them, both his satisfaction in teaching here and his communication with his students. They include such commonplaces as the structure of the academic year and its effect on teaching plans—the division into semesters or quarters, the length of vacations, the existence of summer sessions. The visitors had to learn that the college or university library in this country is quite a different institution from the typical university library elsewhere, whether it belongs to a college of 300 students or a university of 22,000. Student library life was often a mystery to newcomers—reserve shelves, open shelves, interlibrary loans, and the number and kind of books and periodicals available in a particular library. Unexpected were the services the library staff performs for professors and for students.

These matters—not to speak of the need for understanding

the purposes of the American undergraduate college and the students who come to it—often blighted the life of a professor from abroad who had little time to get used to our ways since he was to leave in a year.

ORIENTATION CONFERENCES

Difficulties reported by the Whitney–Fulbright professors, who were encouraged to keep in touch with the Foundation during their time here, led to the suggestion that the Foundation plan a conference with future foreign lecturers, to take place before they commenced teaching. Since each was to teach one semester apiece in two institutions, a representative from each host institution would be invited to attend. It was hoped that the formal discussions of the conference, and the informal conversations that would take place, could give the visitor some sense of what he would encounter, and could help the American sponsor to be useful to the visitor on his campus.

The first Orientation Conference, lasting two days, and designed only for the four Whitney–Fulbright professors, was held in September 1954 at Columbia University. It was conducted to a large extent by members of the Whitney Foundation's Humanities Committee. They were aided by several distinguished American scholars, who were familiar with both American and European education. Together they placed the experiences the visitors would have in the context of the style and purposes of American undergraduate education.

The meeting was so successful and so important, not only for the Whitney–Fulbright professors, but for their American counterparts as well that, on a request from the Conference Board of Associated Research Councils, the Foundation and the Department of State agreed to finance jointly an enlarged orientation conference yearly that would bring to other incoming professors the advantages of the Whitney–Fulbright Conference.

The first enlarged Orientation Conference was held in 1958. Invitations were limited to thirty-five foreign scholars, all here to teach undergraduates, plus American professors from the institutions in which the visitors were to teach. The size of the conference was limited partly because it had limited funds, but it was also deemed important to keep the group small enough to allow free exchange of ideas and provide an environment in which these men and women from all parts of the world, in the few days they would have together, might communicate with each other and with their American hosts as easily as possible.

To begin with, some administrators in American institutions were reluctant to pay the cost of sending an American representative to the conference; in 1958 with thirty-five foreign scholars, the conference was attended by only eleven American institutional representatives. But by 1960 there were as many Americans as visitors. Deans, department chairmen, and professors came. Some institutions sent no representatives while others sent one even though the timing of the conference made it impossible for their visiting professor to be present. Administrators had realized that the conference could accomplish much for the college as well as for the professor.

The program of the enlarged conference was designed by the Foundation through its Humanities Committee and the CIEP. The Humanities Committee had been selected as a band of men and women committed to the educational purposes of the Foundation, highly knowledgeable about American education and American students, themselves able teachers and administrators. The Washington Committee, which sought for the professors and the students the same values the Foundation did, efficiently shared the administrative management, which was as complicated as the creation of the program itself. During the first six years, the conferences were held on the campus of Sarah Lawrence College, where the atmosphere was friendly and unstrained and somehow encouraged, even among people accustomed to formality in their own countries, an easy access to others. The Foundation staff arranged to have visitors met and brought directly to the campus from the New York piers, thirty minutes away, and the airports, forty minutes away. It was a friendly and positive introduction to the life of academic Americans.

The conference lasted four days. Participants discussed in

meetings the nature and structure of the American college and university; the life of college teachers of undergraduates, and their relation to the life of the country as a whole, to their profession, their colleagues, and their students; and the American undergraduate—who he is, why he is at college, what the institution expects of him, and what he expects to get during his life there. There was conversation about the ways of life in an American college, how a professor might function outside his classroom, and much about customs and manners that can be puzzling to a foreigner.

Many conversations took place outside the scheduled sessions of the conference. One visitor wrote: "What I most enjoyed was to be able to meet American professors and scholars casually at meals, or informal discussion groups. I was able to ask them the particular questions I had in mind and the answers were always friendly and helpful."

Americans also commented on the usefulness to them of the brief association, of the opportunity to discuss American education and American culture not only with the visitors but also with their colleagues from this country.

One American said that the chance to talk with the visitor coming to his university permitted them to dispose of a host of questions that are not always clear in correspondence. Being able to clear the ground in advance of his arrival was of mutual advantage to him and to the university.[1]

HOW THE WHITNEY–FULBRIGHT PROGRAM WORKED OUT

Between 1951 and 1965, when the Foundation terminated the Whitney–Fulbright program, professors who received the joint awards came to the United States from the United Kingdom, the Netherlands, Belgium, Italy, France, Germany, Austria, Denmark, Sweden, Finland, Turkey, Egypt, India, Pakistan, China, Japan, the Philippines, Australia, Chile, Brazil, and Argentina.

Imagination and planning, not only for the Orientation

---

1. A fuller account of the Orientation Conferences is given in *The Fulbright Professor Meets the American College*, the John Hay Whitney Foundation, 1962, pp. 11–35.

Conference, but throughout the year, made the teaching experience here valuable for scholars and colleges alike. The Conference Board of the Associated Research Councils in Washington (the parent of CIEP) gave a great deal to the program; Dr. Elizabeth Lam of the CIEP and Georgene Lovecky of the Whitney staff worked with the colleges and the visitors to arrange visits to other institutions, lecture programs at other colleges, and attendance at professional meetings.

Many American institutions, certainly in the 1950s, began by being unaware of the great variety of ways in which men and women from other parts of the world could enrich the lives of individual students, the college itself, and the community, but time after time reports told of the development of new ideas about how the talents of the visitors could be used.

What some of these Whitney–Fulbright professors did illustrates how the presence of foreign scholars as teachers enriched the education of our students. The accounts here are not selected because of any particularly dramatic character—they are representative of the variety of experiences foreign professors had under the Whitney–Fulbright Program. Many original and imaginative consequences flowed from the visiting professorship, beyond those planned or anticipated and beyond the ordinary academic ones.

An African professor, pausing in New York on his way home after a two-year stay in an institution in the South, remarked that he had established a museum of African arts in the college in which he had been teaching. He had written to appropriate individuals all over Africa, and examples of sculpture, carving, and other arts were now on their way to this country. He also mentioned that he had arranged with a colleague at home to come here for a year so that the program of African studies he had instituted could be placed on a solid footing. He was not able to extend his own stay beyond the two years because of demands at home.

The arrangements at the University of Arkansas for Professor Cesar Cecioni, Whitney–Fulbright lecturer in 1955–56, illustrates how a university can draw upon the foreign academic background and field of specialization of a visiting scholar to enrich—not duplicate—course offerings. Professor Cecioni, at the time of his award, was assistant to the Chair of English Language and Literature at the University of Florence. His field of specialization was comparative philology, especially English philology. He suggested, however, that his courses be chosen from a list of six specific titles in the general field of Italian civilization. From these, the university chose Italian–English Literary Relations in the Sixteenth Century and Political Thought from Dante to Machiavelli, the latter jointly sponsored by the departments of philosophy, history, and government. The provost wrote:

> We would also hope that he could serve as guest lecturer occasionally in our courses in European History, 19th Century Literature, World Literature, and Western Civilization. The two courses last named have enrollments of several hundred students in each. These could meet in assembly for his lectures. In addition, we would hope to bring him into personal contact with many students participating in the honors program and with members of our faculty.

At the end of October Dr. Cecioni attended the Southern Modern Language Association meetings at the University of Texas. He wrote:

> The meeting was both interesting and enjoyable and gave me the opportunity to see the big heart of Texas and the great University of Austin which is really impressive. The meeting was a large one (about 370 people) and I could speak to teachers coming to Austin from several parts of the South (Mississippi, Alabama, Louisiana, Oklahoma, etc.). I received several invitations to give occasional lectures in several places and shall do my best to do it as far as possible, although I cannot spend my time going around without neglecting my duties here, which I do not want to do. Almost all these people are prepared to meet my travel expenses, but

there are two small colleges (one in Oklahoma and the other in Louisiana), which seemed quite excited (I mean their representatives in Austin, not the colleges) at the idea of having such an opportunity, but made me also understand that they were rather hard up and could not afford it. You will perhaps be able to arrange for me to draw on my travel fund for this purpose. I shall be much happier to do it for these places which apparently never have seen a European professor in their life than for other institutions which can easily afford a Visiting Professor as soon as they want one.

A number of lectures in and out of Arkansas grew out of these associations—lectures in small colleges, teachers colleges, and universities. He reported:

I was particularly impressed with the eagerness and interest of the students and the people in Arkadelphia. The lecture was delivered in a theater which was literally crowded. The day before I had attended an informal gathering of the students in the Department of English as a sort of preparatory meeting and several topics concerning contemporary Italian literature and the social and political problems of Italy and Europe were discussed.

Dr. Cecioni spent the Christmas vacation in South Carolina:

There I was the guest of Professor Duncan Eaves, a well-known scholar of Southern Literature and the editor of the letters of W. C. Simms. My trip was really a rewarding experience—altogether, when I go back to Europe I shall be an authority on the South of the United States. From South Carolina I went to Chicago for the Modern Language Convention and had the most wonderful time. The meeting was absolutely terrific; more than 2500 people—all American universities and colleges of some standing had their delegation, and I had an opportunity of meeting old friends and making new acquaintances. This, too, was a real experience of American academic life.

Professor Cecioni was through in Arkansas at the end of the first semester. His second teaching appointment was to Rollins College in Florida. Rollins is on the quarter system, and the third quarter opened after the middle of March. Between the end of January and the opening of the Rollins term, he was free for other educational activities. The Conference Board arranged to have him spend February and part of March in Florida, for periods ranging from four to fourteen days, at Stetson University, Bethune-Cookman College, the University of Florida, and Miami University.

Before leaving the country Professor Cecioni was invited to visit Harvard to discuss with interested men there a plan Harvard was working out to establish an Institute for American Studies at the University of Florence, his home university.

On the state of American studies in Italy, Professor Cecioni wrote:

> As ... American studies have been in Italy at a very low ebb for a long time, I think it advisable that the American Commission in Italy should do everything they can to improve the situation, featuring the exchange of professors and students in these fields, sponsoring direct cooperation between American and Italian universities, endowing USIS and university libraries with books and scholarly material, and exerting pressure on the Italian Government for the improvement of the Institute of English and American Literature in Italian universities. In this connection I take the liberty of putting particular emphasis on the importance of the programme of cooperation between the University of Harvard and the University of Florence.

When he was again teaching in his own university, Professor Cecioni wrote that a scholarship had been arranged for a student from his university to study at the University of

Arkansas, and arrangements were being made for a professor from the University of Arkansas to teach in Italy.

The University reported at the conclusion of his stay:

Mr. Cecioni offered a seminar entitled Literary Relations between Italy and England in the Sixteenth Century. This course attracted an enrollment of seventeen graduate students and four undergraduates, the majority of them English majors. It not only gave them a chance to learn material which none of our regular courses offer; even more important it showed them the methods of teaching which are used in continental universities, where the advanced courses are organized and planned quite differently from those in American universities; it taught them the research approach of European seminars; and it brought them into contact with a new way of thinking and with new attitudes and fields of knowledge. . . .

His course in the history of political theory filled an important gap here and gave a new historical perspective; especially, coming from a foreigner it helped to correct nationalistic limitations. . . .

Mr. Cecioni contributed extensively to the intellectual and social life of the University community through public lectures, guest lectures in several courses, talks before various organizations, attendance at University social functions, and wide acquaintanceship and association with individual students, faculty members, and townspeople. . . .

We feel that Mr. Cecioni's stay on our campus has been of great benefit both to our students and to our faculty. Because of our geographical location and our limited budget, we have little opportunity to have foreign scholars in residence. Having Mr. Cecioni here has helped to combat the natural tendency toward provincialism which such circumstances encourage.

The University of Arkansas four years later invited him to return as a visiting lecturer.

To the surprise of many of the visitors, placement in a small university or college far from a metropolitan area was a rewarding and highly satisfactory experience. The vitality of faculty and community relationships was novel to them and more than compensated for missed cultural advantages of a large city. Such was the experience of the Noshy family in Grand Forks, North Dakota. In the nomination of Dr. Ibrahim Noshy in 1955–56, the Fulbright Commission in Egypt chose a leading Egyptian author in classical history and an internationally known historian of Ptolemaic Egypt. He had formerly been dean of the faculty at Ibrahim University and was interested in studying aspects of university administration as well as teaching.

The University of North Dakota was given the opportunity of receiving him since it had expressed strong interest in having a lecturer from the Near East or the Orient. Egypt at that time was in the daily news and the university was confident that there would be general interest in hearing about the Near East from someone directly from Egypt. Dean R. B. Witner wrote: "We are a little off the beaten path and having such a man on our campus should help us and permit us to make some valuable contributions to neighboring schools. I believe his presence on the campus and in this area will help meet a great need." Dr. Noshy was asked to teach two courses: The Ancient Orient and Greece, and Ptolemaic Egypt.

This was indeed an intercultural experiment and a boundary-stretching experience for him and his American hosts. Dr. Noshy, his French-born wife, and their two children approached this assignment in a state university in a small town on the cold northern plains of North Dakota with some trepidation. It meant a radical change from their life in the sophisticated metropolis of Cairo. It was not easy for them to get accustomed to unfamiliar housekeeping responsibilities and life without servants. Many of our folkways seemed strange as well. As they got to know the faculty of the university, they were astonished to find congenial colleagues of broad educational experience and cultivated spirit. The warmth of human relations and the many opportunities offered each member of the family to participate in the community brought unexpected satisfactions. Mr. Noshy spoke to a considerable number of community organizations and at four neighboring colleges. Mrs. Noshy gave talks, especially on Egyptian women, to community groups and churches; the two children, aged nine and fourteen, adjusted easily and well in the public schools.

The mutual respect and friendship which emerged from these contacts was no less surprising to the community than to the Noshys. At the conclusion of their stay the Rotary Club of Grand Forks prepared a special eight-page booklet of messages from leaders of the community:

> During his stay in this community, Dr. Noshy has given several lectures throughout the state acquainting our people with the great efforts Egypt is making today to develop its economic resources, overcome its social problems, and expand its educational system.
>
> Dr. Noshy's sincerity and enthusiasm convince us that Egypt will be soon again playing a leading role in world commerce and international peace. . . .
>
> Both in small groups in Grand Forks homes and in the varied functions of our churches and clubs, Dr. Ibrahim Noshy has given unstintingly of his wonderful scholarship. By his life among us, Dr. Noshy has given us a high regard for an interest in his religion of Islam, which he has graciously explained and discussed in study groups.
>
> This talented Egyptian family have, in the few short months, given the citizens of our community an excellent picture of all phases of Egyptian life and culture. Their enthusiasm for their country is unlimited.

When the time came for them to leave Grand Forks for the University of Cincinnati they did so with great reluctance. Dean Witner wrote: "As evidence of the impact they had on our community I was very pleased to see some 15 or so people at the train to see them off. Approximately half of them were townspeople."

Colleges unable to appoint foreign lecturers for a full year, or even a semester, would find possibilities in the kind of program arranged for Professor Pierre Chevrillon of France for one month in 1958–59 at Trinity University, San Antonio, Texas, sandwiched between his first semester at the University of Missouri and the spring quarter at the University of Utah. An intensive schedule was set up of class lectures, public addresses, individual conferences with students, informal student and faculty gatherings in faculty homes, and varied community contacts. Special events focusing on French literature, art, and drama were arranged in the university and in the city. For example, he gave a lecture on the French Impressionists at the McNay Art Institute and participated in the formal opening at the Art Institute of an exhibit: Paris–New York: Painting in the Nineteen-Fifties. The annual student Frolics of Hearts was planned with a "French flavor" in his honor.

He lectured on French literature—on Camus as playwright, on Sartre, and on Paul Valéry; on modern French drama, the psychological novel in France, and French Romanticism. And he spoke on education in France and his impressions of education here. He spoke on De Gaulle and France. The students wrote in their newspaper:

> Thank you scarcely seems an adequate phrase to express appreciation for M. Pierre Chevrillon's exciting series of lectures. It can, however, symbolize gratitude for the tantalizing taste these all-too-brief lectures have afforded. The Chevrillon Lectures reflect the philosophy long held by Trinity that education involves the pursuit, grasp and utilization of ideas. The lectures are surely timely; for it is this philosophy that recently has been found inadequate in American Education. M. Chevrillon comes to us as a representative of a nation whose ideas are represented in all phases of our lives.... His lectures have been magic casements through which philosophic and artistic ideas have been traced, examined, and interrelated. We feel fortunate to have participated in these lectures; one hopes that future Trinitonians will have the advantage of a longer series; merci, M. Chevrillon, et au revoir.

The placement of Professor Eulalia Maria Lahmeyer Lobo, a distinguished young historian from the University of Brazil, at the University of Texas the first semester of 1960–61 and at Occidental College the second, was due to the long and active contact which these two institutions had had with South America. Her assignment at Texas was just one course in the history of Brazil—in order to permit her to lecture in neighboring colleges to which no previous Fulbright lecturer had been assigned but where there was much contact at the student level with Latin America: Arlington State College, Texas Agricultural and Mechanical, Rice University, the University of Houston, the Agricultural and Mechanical College, and San Antonio College. Reports on these lectures repeatedly reflect the enthusiasm with which she was received.

Her account of her visit at Texas A&M College at Prairie View, a Negro state college, vividly communicates the values of such an experience to the foreign lecturer. After her talk, she reports, the discussion, which did not end until 2 A.M., was extremely lively and intellectually stimulating, and gave a vivid image of the concerns of the students in the college. Their greatest interest was in integration. They asked searching questions about how this issue is dealt with in Brazil, a country in which the mingling of races has a long history. Six months after this lecture, on her return to New York, Dr. Lobo was still greatly impressed by the seriousness with which the students probed this disturbing question, the intelligence with which they approached the problems it presented, and their eagerness to learn whatever they could from another country that might throw light on their own.

Her assignment at Occidental College gave her an opportunity to become an active and integral member of the teaching staff of a liberal arts college. Dean Bollman wrote:

> Students, faculty, administration, and members of the community were most enthusiastic about the teaching and lecturing of Dr. Lobo. She is an outstanding scholar in her field and contributed significantly to our educational program during her term with us both in the Department of History and in our general education program.

Dr. Lobo is an articulate and extremely knowledgeable ambassador of her native country, Brazil. Her scholarly lectures on a wide variety of topics were praised and commended by all who attended.

Dr. Lobo gave speeches before campus groups of students, before the Faculty Club, and to many groups in the community. She spoke to the World Affairs Council at Carmel, California, and attended the Fulbright Conference at the California Institute of Technology in Pasadena. Dr. Lobo gave unselfishly of her time, often speaking and discussing her subject until nearly midnight.

Professor Lobo's perceptive comments on her teaching experience illustrated the problems and possibilities of this approach to area studies at the undergraduate level. They reveal both the difficulties she encountered in developing new courses and the changes in her own point of view that the experience brought about:

The professional benefits gathered in this experience of teaching in the United States seem to me invaluable.

First of all to elaborate a program adequate for foreign students, the visiting professor has to proceed to a reappraisal of the relative position of Latin America in the world scenery and is able to do so free from the direct influence of his own milieu.

Secondly, since Latin America, despite the fundamental differences among the various countries, is considered as a block in the United States, I was led to develop the study of under-development which in my opinion accounts for most of the superficial common features of the history of this area.

The concept of underdevelopment and the scale of values derived from it brought about interesting discussions with the students which are familiar only with an economy of full development.

I had also interesting meetings with economists of the University of Texas and the University of Southern

California, who helped me to achieve better means to convey these ideas to the students. Now I am writing on this subject as a request from a French specialized periodical.

Thirdly, the common prejudices of the North American University students about Latin America led also to clarifying discussions both for them and for me, specially the debates about the Catholic religion and its historical function, the Jesuit system of education and the geographical factor (many students still believe in geographical determinism).

On account of the lack of knowledge of foreign languages, the scarcity of works of Latin American scholars translated into English, the difficulties for direct contact with countries of that area, the North American student tends to pass a judgment (since at that age most people feel obliged to judge), on Latin America, on the basis of information furnished almost exclusively by North American historians. Unfortunately, the most outstanding among these write mainly monographs; there is a lack of general works giving a complete coverage of Latin American history. Furthermore text-books generally present Latin America not as such, but under the North American point of view and in relation to the United States. Professor Lewis Wanke, in his book *Latin America, a Continent in Ferment* (Anvil Collection, Montreal, 1939) is the only one I know of who selects and translates excerpts of Latin American historians on the topics he is dealing with, in his text. It is wrong, in my opinion, to try to minimize the differences between Latin America and the United States, they are important, should be recognized as such and understood in order to achieve a fruitful interchange. Therefore it is indispensable to use all means: translation of books, foreign visiting professors, fellowships, teaching of languages to give to the students access to Latin culture if the teaching of history is going to serve any practical purpose in the relationships between Latin America and the United States.

Other professional benefits derived from my visit to the United States comprehend the discussion of teaching methods, curriculum, opportunities to obtain new visual aid material. The flexibility of the North American system of higher education gives room to fruitful debates, as, for instance in the meeting on American Higher Education at the Far Western Conference of Fulbright Scholars, at the California Institute of Technology.

The experience of Dr. Aloo Dastur was quite different from Dr. Lobo's. A political scientist from India, she was most interested in learning about the political process in the United States and managed to observe an extraordinary amount of political activity on the local, state, and national level. She was particularly glad to come to this country in an election year, and attended political meetings and activities carried on by political parties:

> I was fortunate that the elections turned out to be so exciting.... The party alignments and fissures in Congress have taught me much. I went to Washington but on the days I was there Congress was not in session. Anyway I watched Committee proceedings. I intend to go there again next month when we are closed for Easter if it is in session. I saw the workings of the West Virginia State Legislature at Charleston. I shall go to Indianapolis and, if possible, to Springfield, Illinois, for a similar study. During the Easter vacation I intend going to New York to watch the General Assembly and some U.N. Committees at work.

Dr. Dastur was also interested in interpreting her own country to Americans. During the first semester at the University of West Virginia, she taught a course on the Indian Constitution and Constitutional Development in India, and one on Asian Nationalism; she managed also to lecture at other institutions. She was invited to speak at Kent State, in Ohio, and at Emory University, and gave two lectures at Ann Arbor. She participated at Emory University at an "Indian

Week End" planned by another Fulbright Scholar from India stationed at the University. When she completed her semester at West Virginia Dr. Dastur wrote: "My first semester has been very fruitful both as regards my own scheme of study and my teaching. I had a fine batch of students, responsive and critical, young people who were willing to learn and revise, or study, certain pet notions."

Activities at Valparaiso University in Indiana made her appointment there for the second semester particularly timely. The dean wrote to the Conference Board, which planned these appointments, about Dr. Dastur's expected contribution:

As you know, a number of institutions in Indiana have been deeply concerned the past two or three years about the need to encourage study in non-Western areas. President Kretsmann and our faculty have pledged their fullest cooperation to this enterprise. Only recently we received word of a foundation grant, part of which will assist us in building up library holdings in this area.

THE NON-WESTERN SCHOLARS

The Whitney–Fulbright program during most of its existence brought principally European scholars to this country. During the late fifties and early sixties interest in non-Western studies began to grow, and grew rapidly, all over the country. In view of what has happened since, it is hard to remember how limited were the studies involving the Far East in almost all American institutions. In the early 1960s the Commission on International Relations had turned its attention to non-Western studies, and instituted several surveys of the offerings in colleges and universities in this field. At that time there was in fact a marked expansion of non-Western studies in graduate schools, but this had little effect on undergraduate studies. Only one undergraduate institution utilized the funds for area and language study provided by Title VI of the National Defense Education Act during the first six years of its operation. But in 1964, 242 member colleges of the Association of American Colleges reported that they were introducing courses involving non-European life. In its desire to accelerate professional exchanges in the newly important area of education, the Conference Board of Associated Research Councils sought the aid of the John Hay Whitney Foundation, and the Foundation increased to eight the number of its exchange professorships for 1963–64 and nine for 1964–65 in order to give more emphasis to the Far East. Priority in appointments was given to institutions or clusters of institutions that gave some serious indication of interest in developing non-Western studies, and, as before, to institutions in the South and West.

TERMINATION

The Whitney–Fulbright program was brought to a close in 1965. In thirteen years seventy-five foreign professors from twenty-seven countries had received grants and had taught in more than a hundred American colleges.

The academic world is in a far different situation from what it was in 1950 with regard to studies of cultures other than our own, and the interchange of teachers, research scholars, and students has been part of the process by which the world has been continually shrinking. The Foundation program, small as it appeared to be as one watched it from one year to another, made in the end a sizable contribution to the process.

It is easy to overlook the impact of a single Whitney–Fulbright professor, or to think of the total impact as small because the number is small. But this group of men and women had close association with scores of American professors and other citizens. Moreover, the experience of other Fulbright scholars who teach has been similar. Perhaps the more profound implications of the foreign lecturer program from the American point of view is to be sought not only in terms of the intellectual content of their courses but also in the subtler changes in our point of view which they have helped to bring about.

Shining through the reports of the Whitney–Fulbright scholars on their years here are many clues as to what they have thought significant to themselves in their American experiences: the vitality and alertness of their students, the cordial relations of students to faculty and of faculty to townspeople, the warm reception they met at professional meetings, the service functions of the state university.

The need to restate their subject matter for a different audience must have led many of the visitors to reconsideration and re-evaluation. Professor Ninomiyo, from Japan wrote:

> I have, thanks to the actual contact with the unpreoccupied eye of my American students, been made aware of the necessity of re-evaluating our literature in the context of world literature. So far practically no contribution from native scholars has been made to this task.

Part Three

THE WHITNEY
VISITING PROFESSORS

Chapter 13

THE WHITNEY
VISITING PROFESSORS

THE PURPOSE OF THE PROGRAM

The Whitney Visiting Professors Program began 1952. The introduction to its first report (1954) said:

Increasingly the life and culture of people the world over are being shaped by man's control over things physical. The bases of human action in terms of moral and ethical values which constitute the backbone of the humanities have been lost sight of or purposely ignored.

As a consequence, man has failed thus far to devise ways and means for the wise employment of the vast power which science has bestowed upon him. Moreover, with some exceptions, he has failed to realize that many of the vexing problems confronting the individual and society are often highly charged with emotional, ethical and aesthetic factors that do not yield to the familiar types of scientific analysis. To understand the background of these problems and to discover formulas for their solution, one must have recourse to the humanities, for the humanities more than any other discipline are concerned with human thought, feelings, and activity. Not only does acquaintance with the humanities broaden our perspective and deepen our understanding of ourselves and our society, but it equips us with the means of better comprehending and understanding cultures and ways of life alien, and often conflicting, to our own. It is difficult, therefore, to exaggerate the importance of re-emphasizing the study of the humanities at a time when the United States is called upon to exercise humanistic leadership in those expansive areas of the Eastern Hemi-sphere now swept by revolutionary change.

These words were a statement of faith—faith that the United States had an important function to perform in the revolutionary changes going on in other parts of the world, faith that it would indeed exercise humanistic leadership, that education was a critical factor in ensuring the fulfillment of this purpose, and that directing the attention of schools and colleges to the importance of strengthening the study of the humanities was the way to strengthen moral and social values for the task. In the twenty years that followed, this faith has had many blows. The mission seems much less certain, the ways of fulfilling it much cloudier; but the need for strengthening the values that prompted the program is even more urgent now than it was then.

As the accounts in this book of the origins and development of the John Hay Whitney Foundation and its programs attest, this major purpose and this faith were responsible for the style and character of the Foundation, for the individuals chosen to administer the programs, for all the activities the Foundation engaged in.

Like all the Whitney programs, the Visiting Professors project called for direct action in terms of what the Foundation believed needed doing if we were to fulfill our role as a nation. This program's particular function was to enrich and deepen the humanities for undergraduate students by giving them a unique opportunity to study with men and women who represented the best in humanistic education, who had spent long years in university teaching to that end, and who were now invited to spend a year after their retirement in a new place, with new students.

The Foundation saw the increasing difficulty of providing distinguished teachers for the growing population of students, and saw the particular burdens that small, independently sup-ported liberal arts colleges were carrying in trying to maintain and improve teaching in the face of rapidly rising costs and enrollment. It was the interest of the Foundation to create a situation in which students and faculty in such colleges could meet and work with gifted and distinguished teachers, and it proposed to pay the salary of a few such teachers, usually for the first year after retirement, to teach at institutions that could not afford to appoint them. The plan would bring an important man or woman to a campus for a year, and thus give the able teacher, who wanted to continue teaching, a year more of his professional life. It had its practical correlate: "to conserve instructional manpower at a time of expanding student enrollment and teacher shortage in our institutions of higher learning."

This program, like the Whitney–Fulbright Professors' Program, recognized that some of the largest, most distinguished, and most prosperous institutions (and perhaps those with a history of concern for humanistic values) were the best source for such teachers. The plan required the involvement of the Foundation in the selection of both retiring professors and of the colleges they were to go to, and in the way these guest appointments functioned. The Humanities Committee of the Foundation[1] made the selections; the staff, under the direction of Georgene Lovecky, the secretary in charge of the program, worked with the professor and the college in overseeing and assisting with practical arrangements, and the committee and the staff together followed the progress of the assignments throughout the life of the program. Often both teacher and institution turned to the Foundation for counsel and help with particular problems, personal or academic.

HOW THE PROGRAM WORKED

Colleges and universities were notified, and nominations were made for the professorships at the beginning of each academic year, by the president, dean, or department chairman, of men and women who would be retiring that year. Officers of learned societies were also invited to make nominations. As in the case of the John Hay Fellows Program, candidates did not apply or nominate themselves; and, from the beginning, nominators were urged to name only people who met

---

1. A list of the men and women who served on the Humanities Committee will be found on p. xxiv. Not all these individuals served all the time, but most of them served through a large part of the life of this program.

high standards as teachers and scholars. The Selection Committee also had to depend on the nominators to find people who wanted to continue teaching and whose ability to continue teaching was high.

When recommendations were in, the nominee was asked if he wished to be a candidate. The conditions of the appointment were made clear: he would teach in one of the institutions on the Foundation's list; he would have a chance to select the one he preferred from among those that wanted a teacher in his field, but he could not go outside the list—the Foundation was as interested in providing for a particular group of colleges as it was in providing for a particular teacher. If he accepted he was given the opportunity to add letters of recommendation to those already on file.

At the beginning of the academic year, also, the small liberal arts colleges on the Foundation's eligible list were asked whether they were interested in receiving a visiting professor the following year, and in what fields. If they were interested, they were asked what the visitor would teach, where he would live, how he would be involved in the life of the institution. It was the task of the Humanities Committee and the Foundation staff to match teachers with colleges. The matching process was a sensitive and difficult one. The college was sent a list of teachers who might be appropriate, and the college was free to choose from that list. The teacher was then offered the post. If he declined, the college was free to choose another candidate, and the individual was given another choice of college, if there was one that wanted somebody in his field. Sometimes an eligible college could not have a visiting professor because none was available in the fields the college had listed; or a very good candidate might not get an appointment because no college asked for a teacher in his field. But by careful management, by correspondence, visits, and telephone conferences, such misses were kept to a minimum.

In the initial years, the Foundation paid the salary of the professor and his transportation, and the host college provided housing without cost. So that he would be free to participate in events on and off campus as he wished, have time to get to know his students and his colleagues, the Visiting Professor was to teach no more than nine hours a week, although the normal schedules in many of these colleges were heavier.

WIDENING THE PROGRAM

The John Hay Whitney Foundation, in the year this program began, was already sponsoring the John Hay Fellows Program, the Opportunity Fellowship Program, and the Whitney–Fulbright Visiting Professor Program. It was able to appoint six Visiting Professors each of the first two years.

In the second year the number of appointments increased. The New York Foundation became interested:

We believe that this program is fostering a new and practical way of adding to our intellectual capital. Brilliant teachers are among our greatest asset. Anything we can do to conserve these assets and strengthen our colleges today is of great importance. It is for this reason that we are pleased to cooperate in this venture.

The New York Foundation made it possible to add five or six more Visiting Professors each year, on the average, by contributing funds, and also by suggesting that the host college share in paying the professor's salary. It was proposed that the colleges contribute according to their ability. Institutions responded very positively to this request; the amount they contributed varied from a small fraction to one-half the salary. The New York Foundation participated yearly until 1962.

The Humanities Committee enlisted the interest of the Danforth Foundation, which also contributed to the program for four years, adding about four appointments each year.

THE VISITORS—WHERE THEY CAME FROM,
WHERE THEY WENT

Seventy of the Visiting Professors came from large universities, and 54 from medium-sized universities and small colleges; 57 of the 124 came from places in the Northeast, 65 from institutions in the Middle West, the West, and the South; 2 came from foreign universities.

No appointments were made to large universities. All were made to institutions with fewer than 1,500 undergraduates, many to colleges with 500 to 1,000 students; 41 professors were appointed to colleges in the Northeast, 83 to colleges in the Middle West, the West, and the South. A few colleges were on both the contributing and the receiving ends of the program, but this was exceptional.

As in the case of the Whitney–Fulbright Professors Program, the Foundation's advisers had in mind at the beginning that visiting professors were most needed by the smaller colleges in the Middle West, the West and the South, and most of them went to these parts of the country, but the figures indicate that a substantial minority went to colleges in the Northeast.

The original assumption—that the professors would go to liberal arts colleges struggling with inadequate resources to build a faculty—guided the selection of colleges. But, as in other cases, the Foundation was flexible. Occasionally a better-endowed college had a particular need which its budget could not meet, even though the budget was generally adequate. So the range of colleges to which professors went, in terms of their academic quality and the nature and degree of their financial need, was quite wide. They ranged from the southern college whose budget allowed only $250 a year for science equipment, to a small college with a reputation for high academic standards and a quality faculty, which needed funds for a particular appointment to get some new studies under way, that its budget did not allow, and for which an experienced older scholar was needed.

Who were the Visiting Professors? Some were of national and international reputation, some unknown outside their professional circle. But all had a long history of exceptional teaching and concern for students, and had a genuine interest in moving for a year to a different part of the country, with a different academic environment and perhaps quite different kinds of students than they had previously known.

They knew they were not undertaking the life of a secluded scholar—the conditions of appointment meant that they would become part of the life of the institution and, to some degree, of the community; few of the colleges were in large urban centers, and the kind of anonymity possible in a cosmopolitan environment would not be available.

The subjects they taught covered the range of a normal undergraduate curriculum—the arts, literature, the classics, philosophy, history, political science, economics, sociology, anthropology, psychology. Of the 124 appointments, the largest number were in history, English and American literature, and foreign languages and literature, with the arts, philosophy, and the classics next. There were seven appointments in science and mathematics.

HOW THEY FUNCTIONED

With students. While one of the important reasons for this program was the opportunity it gave an active teacher to continue teaching, and the personal satisfaction this experience might give him, perhaps even more important was what his presence might do for the college and the students in it. The record of the kinds of services performed gives an interesting picture of the visiting professor and of the response of students, the needs of the institution, and the imagination of the administration and faculty of the host college.

Mentioned more often than any other quality was the visitor's success in stimulating the students, and his availability to them. One cannot help being moved by the evidence—in statements by students, by administrators and faculty, and by the professors themselves—of high energy and the willingness to spend it, at the end of a long career, on a new group of students in a new situation. These are men and women in their late sixties and early seventies, and there is a remarkably youthful quality in their response to students and the ways they discovered for communicating with them.

A student at Knox College reported how profoundly Professor John Collier had altered his outlook on the social sciences, and, indeed, the shifts and changes the professor had

had to make to accommodate the students who wanted to study with him. His course on the Indians of America had been limited to twenty-eight students; it had to be repeated in the second term and fifty-four students were permitted to register. It was the same story with a seminar on anthropology and conservation. While the high and stimulating quality of his teaching came first, important relations with students typically went beyond the classroom. An administrator wrote of him:

> He gave us the impression of being a quiet, very busy person, working on his courses and the research related to them. He was a person who did not particularly seek social contacts, but who nevertheless became very appealing to the students, who discovered that they in turn were very warmly received by him. By the end of the winter quarter students were seeking him out at his residence and obviously deeply appreciated him for his personal as well as for his professional qualities.

About his associations with students at Hamilton College, Clarence Hamilton, who came from Oberlin wrote:

> Of these students I have come to know a good number personally and have had consultations with them, especially with those taking up the study of philosophical and religious subjects for the first time. In the smaller class it has been easier to have more contact. On nights when the young men read their term papers on different great religions, the class meets in my home. Fortunately the house provided by Hamilton College has a commodious living room, beautifully furnished, with a large fireplace where, on these wintry evenings, we can sit about a blazing fire and discuss under agreeable circumstances. In the midst of the evenings Mrs. Hamilton serves refreshments while the discussion continues. From these sessions I hope the students will carry away memorable and happy impressions associated with the extensive themes we have before us.

About his own response to the students he writes:

> All in all, I find this the most profoundly satisfying year of the many in my teaching experience. After preoccupation with specialized studies in graduate schools, which had largely been my lot, it is both stimulating and rewarding to teach courses to eager youth at the undergraduate level. It draws upon all sides of one's experience and thought, and affords an opportunity to bring into grand perspective many things known separately before. At least teaching the history of philosophical and religious thought does that. Something of the same experience seems to happen to the students also. I have been impressed by the fact that in spontaneous comment on my courses they mention more frequently than anything else that they now see a wider significance in many things they learned before as isolated segments of information. That happens, I suppose, because one cannot study the story of the religions and philosophies of the world without becoming aware of the history of civilization itself. At any rate it is most gratifying to know that they feel something of the eternal marvel of man's search for the higher life.

With the departments. Some professors stimulated the development of a new department or revived an old one. Roger Rusk, professor of physics at Mount Holyoke, spent a year at Furman University in South Carolina. The university had just moved from a small, inadequate campus to a new one, and was actively engaged in improving itself. Rusk found only one professor of physics at the university, and much of the equipment broken and out of date. The mathematics and physics teachers welcomed his coming and the help he would give in rejuvenating the department. He made a survey of science departments in the South, and his report quickly brought $7,000 from the university for new equipment. "This may not seem much," he wrote, "but, in comparison with the $250 per year the department had been running on, it was magnificent, and we at once made the best use of it." He worked with the small faculty to rewrite the experiments in the general course and brought experience and ideas that helped them introduce new experiments, almost doubling the number; they re-established lecture demonstrations, with which little had been done, and made a start at putting laboratory experiments into a course in atomic and nuclear physics.

"His influence has worked a revolution in the Division of Sciences," wrote the Dean of Furman about Rusk's presence on the campus. "Often I have heard the question 'What has happened over at the Science Building to change things so?' Enrollment in physics classes jumped. We have had more students majoring in physics since he came than we have had in years."

Thiel College asked for W. C. Ronan, professor of architecture at Ohio State, because it wanted help in developing an art department. He helped the college start a slide collection, made most of the recommendations for purchases of new books, and greatly stimulated the people responsible for carrying out the plan.

Of Professor R. Bryllion Fagin, who went to LeMoyne College from the Johns Hopkins University, the dean wrote:

> He has served as a tremendous stimulus.... As an addition to the English staff per se, he drew unstinting admiration and praise, and he worked hand in glove with the other members of the Department of English in organizing a coherent, well-integrated program of English both for majors and general education students.

The visiting professors were a rich source of help to colleges in developing curricula and their libraries. Professor Hamilton turned over his bibliographies on the major religions of India and the Far East to the Hamilton College Library, which was excellent, he wrote, "but they welcomed these recommendations."

Professor John Alford went to Middlebury College from the Rhode Island School of Design, and worked with faculty on developments in art. The dean wrote:

Near the close of the college year, President Stratton, Vice President Freeman, Professor Alford and I enjoyed a long conference which gave opportunity for us to learn Professor Alford's appraisal of our Fine Arts program. He spoke freely and was generous with suggestions as to ways and means of improving the facilities and operation of the Department. Fine Arts is our youngest department of instruction.

Professor John J. Dashiell, psychologist from the faculty of the University of North Carolina, was appointed to Wake Forest College. At the end of his year there he wrote:

The College had reached that academic milestone when it became realized that the teaching of psychology should be divorced from that of philosophy; and the faculty had voted for the organization of an independent Department of Psychology. It was coincidental that I became retired just at this time. My appointment to the Whitney Professorship was then in a sense timely, as helping to bring an older experienced psychologist and a college needing psychological experience together....

One clear need of the college was a Center for Psychological Services: individual counselling, testing programs, etc. For this I nominated a man who was eventually engaged to set up the Center, and who is impressing everyone most favorably. This is professionalized psychology.

He impressed on the college the need for the study of psychology as a science related to the biological sciences. This supported the views of the biology faculty and the college proceeded to raise funds for a life sciences building to be shared by the two departments. Professor Dashiell had an important part in designing the building itself, and in planning the fixtures and technical equipment for the study of psychology.

Wake Forest appointed Dr. Dashiell acting chairman of the new psychology department for the following year, and appointed a third member to the department. The president reported: "His work with us has been significant in every way. His personal leadership on the campus has been dynamic and cordial. He has cooperated in a fine spirit with faculty, students and administration. His classroom work has been very effective."

With faculty and administration. The importance of the Visiting Professors to the faculty of the host institutions was probably not envisioned in the original planning but turned out to be one of the most valuable consequences of the program.

The Visiting Professorship started Professor Broadus Mitchell on a long post-retirement career. The year after his retirement from the economics faculty at Rutgers University in 1957 he received a Whitney appointment to Hofstra University, then Hofstra College. He was invited to remain for a second year. That summer the Ford Foundation sponsored a workshop at the college to consider the establishment of a small experimental college within the larger one, and Dr. Mitchell was asked to participate. Thus New College was created—an innovative, imaginative institution that took none of the academic conventions for granted—calendar, curriculum, prerequisites, credits, examinations, grades—but examined them all, and examined possible alternatives. It was not to be an "elite" institution but one for the regular Hofstra student who might be interested in a new design for his education. The college was planned in the beginning to make a three-year program possible for students who wanted it. For Professor Mitchell, post-retirement teaching meant not merely carrying on as before, but it also involved the kind of rethinking about basic educational matters sometimes thought to be the prerogative of the young.

After a year Professor Mitchell went on leave to teach in the University of Puerto Rico, returned, and remained on annual appointments until June 1968, when he reached the age of 75. After that he taught, off and on, at Mills College of Education, and finally in 1971, on an emergency appointment, taught for a semester at the University of Rhode Island.

"I came and went by bus," he writes, "my classes being

confined to three days a week." "For the rest," he adds, "I pecked away at the typewriter and managed to publish something in the way of a book every year or two." It is now fourteen years since Professor Mitchell "retired"!

Of Paul Knaplund, who went from the University of Wisconsin to Wells College, the president wrote: "He was an especial inspiration to young faculty," and the record of his impact on faculty in that college as well as on students is impressive.

"I was especially pleased," wrote the Dean of Redlands about Professor Clyde Murley, "that younger members of the faculty sought his advice and counsel on many problems."

Professor M. C. Elmer and his wife, in their year at Western College for Women, had an apartment at a central location on the campus and was particularly valuable in counseling faculty members as well as students.

The willingness and talent of Visiting Professors to serve as advisers on all fronts is conspicuous in the record of their year of teaching. There are many instances of the impact of their wisdom and experience; their concern for the broader aspects of education is attested many times.

> As you know, all too well, some of the most fanatical battleship admirals on many faculties are the younger men who cannot see beyond the confines of their subject matter disciplines and their departments. Our chief reason for wanting highly reputable senior scholars here is to counteract that tendency.

This is Dean Doyle of Washington College in Chestertown, Maryland, apropos Helen Sandison, who came to their English department on retiring from Vassar. And he goes on:

> There is no need to tell you that we are delighted beyond words with the work that Professor Helen Sandison is doing for us. She is teaching in regular required sections, which we feel are the most important classes in the College program. It is in these classes that the majority of academic casualties are caused and it is also

on this level that the department chairmen are far too prone to assign younger instructors when they ought to be teaching these sections themselves. Miss Sandison's presence in these courses is furnishing us with an invaluable yardstick of performance which I believe is going to have a most salutary effect on work right across the board in the most important part of our program.

The next fall Dean Doyle wrote to the Foundation:

We asked her to return to us as a regular faculty member, but were unable to dissuade her from carrying out her plan to spend the year in New York. Our favorable impression of her work was so strong that it was influential in our decision to appoint another emeritus professor, Ray E. Gilman of Brown University, to our Department of Mathematics. I am sure the Foundation will be pleased to know of this by-product of the Whitney appointment.

To many administrators, as well as to faculty, the Visiting Professors were important additions to the campus. After commenting on Professor Sandison's contribution to the faculty Dean Doyle added:

Her relation to the administration was of course the most clearly visible to me. I feel that I myself received so much benefit from her year with us that (quite selfishly) I should say that her support to me was alone worth the whole appointment. As a relatively young administrator, I found it invaluable to have with us a seasoned colleague who had many years of experience as a department chairman and a member of the chief policy-making committees in an excellent institution— and who at the same time was in a visiting status and could not conceivably have any personal ambitions or motives for her advice. I consulted her frequently on the most sensitive and important matters of policy and derived immense reassurance from her suggestions and, needless to say, particularly from her approval of my stands on various issues. I think this kind of opportunity for administrators is something that you could well emphasize in your description of the Foundations appointments.

Professor Harold Bruce went from Dartmouth to Pomona College as Visiting Professor, and of his service to the administration there President Lyon wrote:

His relations with the administration have been intimate and much valued. We have called upon him for information regarding his experiences at Dartmouth, and particularly from his service on the committee which reorganized the Dartmouth curriculum and schedules. Personally, I have consulted him on several matters where the advice of a mature professor from another institution would be very valuable to me. His counsel has always been sound and I have found him a real asset in the administrative problems.

President Everett of Hollins College wrote particularly of the importance of Professor Clair Littell's presence to him, emphasizing the benefit from his aid and guidance. "I spent many hours with him talking over my own problems and he very kindly gave me excellent guidance. The Dean has reported the same situation."

No one reading the record of the activities of the Visiting Professors could conclude that the year of retirement teaching was a let-down year. The teaching schedule of nine hours was not light by current standards, but twelve or fifteen hours was more common in the 1950s than now, and nine hours was thought of as light compared with the normal teaching load in many of the colleges to which the professors went.

In addition, the hope was that the visitors would have outside associations with faculty, students, and administrators, and "become a part of the community." This expectation seems to have been fulfilled with remarkable consistency; and, indeed, a glimpse of some professors' appointment books leaves one a little breathless.

In one rather extreme case the visitor, Professor Cornelia Coulter of Mount Holyoke, after listing her activities, adds:

> Having said all this, I must acknowledge that I have enjoyed my year at Hiram College so much that, even if I had known beforehand just what lay before me, I probably should have accepted just the same....
>
> I simply had in mind that, given a small liberal arts college with high standards, and a Visiting Professor who enjoys teaching and is interested in other activities, on and near the campus...the resulting schedule of appointments may sometimes be heavier than a person aged sixty-five or over ought to undertake.

We might add that the enrollment in her Greek classes was so large that Hiram invited Professor Coulter back for two successive years—on a reduced program, to be sure—and she returned.

One reason that Professor Coulter was more than normally scheduled was the Hiram College "one-course" plan, according to which each student studied one subject for seven weeks. The student had a fifteen-hour schedule, and the teacher did also. No Latin or Greek was being taught at Hiram when Professor Coulter came, and the faculty was most anxious that she should reintroduce them to the curriculum. A professor of education mentioned a junior who needed three extra hours of Latin prose composition for a teaching certificate, and Dr. Coulter agreed to give her a course. One of the faculty most anxious to establish the classics suggested a "classical symposium" with a program of papers, to which people from other parts of Ohio and from Pennsylvania would be invited. She agreed to that also, and ultimately was chairman of the committee on arrangements for the symposium, which went off very successfully.

Professor Orrin Smith, of the DePauw Department of Physics spent a year at Kalamazoo College. He wrote:

There was instituted during the year a series of four or five science division meetings per semester in which methods, attitudes, standards and so forth were discussed quite frankly and informally and with no visible inter-departmental bitterness. The meetings were valuable, well attended, and contributed to interdepartmental un-derstanding and cooperation.

The faculty–town rapport is as good as that in any other college I have known. The city has a high cultural level and the city and its colleges cooperate in many ventures and each seems to take pride in the other.

Kirtley Mather, of Harvard, in his one semester at Carleton College was in great demand as a speaker—he spoke at the annual meeting of the Geology Club of the University of Minnesota, before the Earth Science Club of Rochester, and to Sigma Xi. Frank Kille, then of the biology department at Carleton wrote:

He was community-minded and quickly became a welcome member of the Northfield Community. He spoke in the Methodist Church, the town service clubs, and had high school and townsfolk at his home for social occasions. As one said, "All in all he had a salutary effect on town and gown. I heard many favor-able comments from people in the town." He spoke to the entire student body at St. Olaf College and was well received there.

Our experience with Professor Mather demonstrates without question that when you have the right man, he can make a terrific impact on all members of the college and town communities even though he is present for only one semester.

THE VISITING PROFESSOR IN THE BLACK COLLEGE

In light of the efforts the academic world is now making to improve the education of black students it is likely that if the Visiting Professors Program had begun in 1971 particular thought would be given to its usefulness to the black colleges. With good reason there is concern about the drain of talented black teachers away from black colleges in the South, and the increasing need for good teachers there. If more able retired teachers had gone to the black colleges during the 1950s and early 1960s they might have made a great impact on them at a time when the need was as great as it is now but not so visible.

There were no black retired professors among the 124 who took part in the program. Eleven white professors spent their year at black colleges—Fisk, Spelman, and Bennett each had two, and Morehouse, Tougaloo, Dillard, Virginia Union, and LeMoyne each had one. In addition three men had year appointments to the Richmond University Center, a consortium of five Virginia colleges, some black, some white.

Reflections of his experiences at black colleges are expressed by Professor Fagin, who as mentioned earlier went to LeMoyne College from Johns Hopkins in 1958–59. He wrote:

> The students were eager and hard-working, but rather poorly prepared for college work. The Negro schools in Memphis are overcrowded and understaffed. Fifty-one percent of the teachers are graduates of LeMoyne, most of them dating from the years when LeMoyne had only recently become a senior college, and there is no place for them, west of Nashville, to take any refresher courses on the graduate level....
>
> The lack of preparation was glaring: most of my students were English majors; but I found that names like Dryden or Matthew Arnold or Swinburne rang no bells; that literary movements meant nothing to them; and that none of them had ever seen a production of a play, outside of an isolated high school performance. One must bear in mind that neither the one professional theatre in the city nor the community amateur theatre nor the dramatic clubs of the Memphis State University and Southwestern College will admit Negro auditors. I tried to get permission to send my twelve students enrolled in my Shakespeare class to a performance of *King Lear*

at MSU, but that privilege was denied them. Nor did I succeed in getting permission for them to see the film of *Henry V* with Laurence Olivier at the only movie house in town which imports European films. I finally settled for directing my own class in a production of Shaw's *Dark Lady of the Sonnets*. We put it on at a student and faculty assembly, sans scenery and costumes, but the play came through effectively nonetheless. . . .

LeMoyne is the only institution of higher learning for Negroes in the triangle made up of West Tennessee, North Mississippi and East Arkansas. Its intentions, ideals and aspirations are laudable; its administration is considerate of the students' needs; its faculty contains many dedicated men and women; and its students are youngsters growing intellectually and eager to prepare themselves for leadership among their people, and show a tremendous capacity for acquiring knowledge. I found a few gifted students in my Creative Writing Seminar, and was successful in securing a scholarship to Brandeis University for a student who showed special endowment for work in drama and the theatre, and helped to get a Woodrow Wilson scholarship for another student, an English major, who is now enrolled at Boston University. I am glad that I had the opportunity to serve them to the best of my limited abilities, and I am grateful to the John Hay Whitney Foundation for making it possible for me and them to get together.

Professor V. T. Thayer, whose influence in education throughout the country has been very great, spent a year as Visiting Professor of Education at Fisk University, in Nashville, in 1956–57, during the first phase of activity after the Supreme Court ruling on desegregation. This was before the complexities had fully appeared—while most concerned educators hoped, if they did not quite believe, that integration might make steady progress—and before the movement for black separatism made it clear that deeper and more farreaching procedures would have to be developed to achieve integration than most people had supposed.

Fisk University seemed a favorable place for desegregation. It is one of the most distinguished institutions for black students, one that had always had a small white population, a university with higher academic standards than most black colleges; it had been led for years by Charles Johnson, one of the most intelligent, knowledgeable, and humane educators of his generation. One could expect the administration, faculty, students, and the interested public to press forward toward true integration. Unfortunately, Dr. Johnson's untimely death left the university without the leadership he would have given its new tasks.

The administration's first plan for integration was to attract more white students. But it is even more difficult for an all-black college to become integrated than for an all-white one. Moreover, the admission of black students to graduate schools elsewhere caused a decline in the number of graduate students at Fisk. Dr. Thayer participated in the discussions of these matters and of the proposal that Fisk concentrate on the creation of black teachers and administrators who would be able to take their place in integrated institutions.

Dr. Thayer's year at Fisk came at a critical moment, and his unusual experience in education was fortunate for the university. Describing his year with the students, he wrote:

> The year of contact with them has been at times inspiring, at times frustrating, never dull or uninteresting. They constitute what Reverend King terms the "new Negro," and while a considerable proportion are attending school for no purpose other than to rise in the social scale, many are resolved to prepare themselves to better the status of their race in American society. I leave Fisk with the conviction that, despite the difficulties and problems to which I have referred, the University is contributing significantly to the realization of a sacred mission.

Harvey Stork had a year at Tougaloo Southern Christian College in Mississippi in 1957–58, teaching botany. On completing the year he wrote a piece on the experience of teaching at Tougaloo and on the prejudice, hostility, and fear in the surrounding community—in educational institutions as well as in the community at large:

> I had seen academic freedom made a mockery in a white Methodist college that was called a liberal arts college. One of its alumni, a member of the State Legislature, in a speech is quoted as saying, "They accuse this college of being liberal; I stand ready to defend it against such a charge." ...
>
> In the Jackson Daily News I never saw even a suggestion of the moderate view, in spite of the fact that I met a number of the more thoughtful Jacksonites who were moderates but would not be quoted; you might lose some of your business or professional practice. . . . When Mississippi State College staged the inauguration of a new president, the neighboring college of Tougaloo, but a few miles away, was not asked to send a representative. . . . Many problems in the State for the years ahead were cited by the new president, by the Governor, by the President of the Board, by top educators, by an editor, but nary a reference to any possible overtures to an amelioration of the racial hiatus.

Professor Stork went on to say that perhaps the training of teachers at Tougaloo might have far-reaching effects:

> Most of these people will teach in Mississippi and help strengthen Negro education all down the line. Pre-medicine, pre-law, pre-engineering are important, of course. But too often these graduates, and especially the superior ones, take off for California, Chicago, Detroit, New York. For this I cannot blame them so long as their own state does not give them a fair shake.
>
> Here is a college dedicated not to developing better skills in dairying, cotton and corn farming, poultry raising, house construction, transportation, and the many

facets of that training that will help answer the question of what shall we eat, what shall we wear, how many horsepower shall we drive, but a liberal arts college in the true liberal sense of open wide the windows in all directions toward the best that men have thought and taught and written. Only this can give a sense of direction. From what I read and see, this is a center, and the foremost center in the South. . . . I know of nothing better that could happen to the Southern Negro than the development of a center for the nurturing of a philosophy that would permeate the thinking of the less fortunate half of the population of the State of Mississippi.

THE RICHMOND UNIVERSITY CENTER

Three professors spent the Whitney year with the Richmond University Center, a collaborative arrangement of five Virginia institutions—three white and two black—that joined to support activities no one of them could readily support alone. Several other Visiting Professors lectured for short periods under the auspices of the center.

The experience of Professor Avery Craven of the University of Chicago illustrates how the center functioned. In the course of his year he delivered twenty-two lectures on such topics of particular interest to the South as: "The South and the Democratic Process," "The History of Soil Exhaustion in Virginia," "History in the Age of Fear," "The Academic Man in a Democracy," "The Civil War and the Cold War." These lectures were attended by 450 undergraduates and 50 graduate students. In addition Professor Craven addressed the History Club at the University of Virginia, opened the Arts Festival at Virginia Union University, spoke to meetings of the faculty and of history majors at several of the center's colleges, and lectured at other colleges in and outside the consortium.

This kind of assignment was a digression from the Visiting Professors' plan but had in common with it the idea that teachers such as these could have a particularly important educational function in other than conventional classroom situations.

TERMINATION

This program, begun in 1952, was terminated in 1963, and in the eleven years of its existence awarded Visiting Professorships to 124 retired professors. The New York Foundation participated from 1953 to 1962, the Danforth Foundation from 1957 to 1961.

As the stories of other John Hay Whitney Foundation programs indicate, the middle sixties was a time for reconsideration of all the issues in education in this country. All the Foundation programs had been started at the beginning of the decade of the 1950s and were carried on with a high degree of consistency—the Whitney–Fulbright and Visiting Professors Programs until 1965 and 1963, the John Hay Fellows Program until 1966, and the Opportunity Fellowships Program until 1971–72. The last years of the 1960s were a period of reconsideration by the Foundation of what critical issues need to be dealt with in the 1970s. The result was that all its old programs were concluded, and new ones were begun.

There was a particular reason for terminating the Visiting Professors Program after eleven years. From the late 1950s on, universities became more alert to the possible continuing contributions that could be made by faculty members who reached retirement age. They increasingly kept the best of their retiring faculty on yearly appointments, and began to eye acquisitively the men and women about to retire from other institutions. Universities were sponsoring vastly increasing research projects for which the older scholars were essential.

And, although the private colleges in whose interest the Visiting Professors Program was inaugurated and carried on were still in financial straits, by 1962 or 1963 the more eminent retiring scholars were not. Few needed the Visiting Professors Program, and it was time to close it down.

THE REGISTRY OF RETIRED PROFESSORS

Shortly after the Visiting Professors Program was established, colleges began asking the Foundation if its files contained the names of retired professors who might be interested in an appointment, independent of the program. The Foundation responded to these individual inquiries. As they multiplied, almost of its own momentum an informal registry of names and information about retired professors grew up as an adjunct to the program. It was of course confined to the humanities, broadly conceived. The list contained the names of known persons in particular fields, brief resumés of their education and experience, and references. The Foundation took no part in making selections or recommendations, and all discussions of salary and schedule were left to the colleges and interested teachers.

By 1956 the Registry had grown to such proportions that it became a financial burden—and the service it performed, although important, was peripheral to the interests of the Foundation. It began to seem more appropriate to use the funds absorbed by the Registry for the support of individuals who could participate in the Foundation's programs.

Moreover, other organizations, whose purposes were more strictly in line with the function of the Registry, had interested themselves in the placement of professors. A very large National Registration in the Humanities and Social Sciences was supported by the American Council of Learned Societies. For a small fee academic and governmental organizations were able to get from the ACLS a panel of names from which to make selections.

Also, the American Association of University Professors in 1956 adopted a proposal to establish, if financing could be arranged, a register of retired professors available for teaching positions.

A year earlier the Teachers Insurance Annuity Association had undertaken a study to consider how retired professors might continue to contribute to the academic and intellectual life of the country—a purpose much more inclusive than a registry. Its report recommended a visiting professors program for independent colleges, a research professorship program for independent colleges, and a central registry for retired professors.

The John Hay Whitney Foundation called a meeting in May 1956 of persons from these and other organizations interested in the problem; this meeting indicated both the need for a central registry, administered by a central agency, and also faced realistically the cost of such an enterprise. On the basis of the conclusions of this meeting, and of discussions in the Board of Trustees, it was decided that the Foundation would continue the Registry through 1957, and that in the intervening year information about it would be more widely disseminated in order to stimulate the interest of some more appropriate organization. This was done, and in 1958 the Association of American Colleges and the American Association of University Professors assumed responsibility for the project. The Ford Foundation contributed funds for its support for the first five years. After that it was paid for equally by the AAC, the AAUP, and the TIAA. During the 1960s it became increasingly expensive, however. On the one hand retired professors were increasingly finding ways to use their talents without the assistance of the Registry, and on the other the great teacher shortage was over, with the influx of new Ph.D.s, so the Registry was closed in August 1970.

Appendixes

Appendix A

THE OPPORTUNITY FELLOWS

Abrams, George H. *1968–69* *Anthropology*
Acoya, Andrew *1969–70* Architecture
Adame, Felipe *1970–71* Social Work
Adams, Armenta E. *1958–59* Music
Adams, Charles *1971–72* Medicine
Adams, Samuel C., Jr. *1951–52* Sociol.
Adewale-Mendes, Rose E. M. *1971–72* Law
Adkins, Karl *1968–69* Law
Aguilar, Jose A. *1950–52* Medicine
*Akimoto, Mary Fumi (Schmidt) *1952–53* Dance
Akita, George *1955–57* History
Alers-Montalvo, M. *1953–54* Sociol., Anthro.
Allen, Betty L. *1953–54* Voice
Allen, Samuel E., Jr. *1961–62* History
Allen, Van S. *1950–51* Biology
Alexander, Sandra M. *1971–72* Nursing
Alston, Thaddas L. *1968–69* Law
Amerson, Ralph Waldo *1950–51* Law
Amioka, Shiro *1958–59* Education
Anchondo, Robert L. *1969–70* Law
Anderson, Ned *1967–68* Law
Andrew, Muriel R. *1952–53* Public Admin.
Andrews, Benny *1965–66* Painting
Angel, Frank, Jr. *1950–51* Education
Anthony, Carl C. *1965–66* Architecture
Anthony, Clara B. *1958–59* English
Apodaca, Anacleto G. *1950–51* Education
Applewhaite, Eleanor S. *1961–62* Law
Araki, James T. *1956–57* Oriental Lang.
Archer, Anna Laura *1959–60* Dance
Ardaiz, Amand A. *1969–70* Government
Arriola, Paul M. *1952–53* Spanish
Artero, Margaret T. *1971–72* Education
Artichoker, John, Jr. *1956–57* Education
Arvizu, Rafael *1969–70* Law
Atkins, Thomas I. *1967–68* Law
Austin, Eduardo *1957–58* Political Sci.
Azure, Clement E. *1953–54* Education
Baca, Albert R. *1953–54* Classics
Baca, Reynaldo R. *1970–71* Education
Bailey, Ronald B. *1959–60* Political Sci.
Bailey, Willie Lee *1969–70* Law
Baker, Barbara J. *1968–69* Law
Baker, H. A., Jr. *1965–66* Literature

Baker, William H. *1967–58* Economics
Ball, C. S. Kidwell *1965–66* Hist. of Sci.
Ballard, A. B., Jr. *1955–56* Polit. Sci.
Banks, Esther M. *1955–57* Anthropol.
Banks, Lois E. (Hollis) *1962–63* Political Sci.
Baptiste, Victor N. *1959–60* Spanish
Baquero, Jenaro *1960–61* Economics
Barba, Paul *1971–72* Law
Barbosa, Charles M. *1957–58* Education
Baraka, Imamu Amiri (Leroi Jones) *1961–62* Writing
Barnes, Edward J. *1956–57* Psychology
Barrera, Hebe *1965–66* English
Barrera, Nickolas S. *1963–65* Law
Barrett, Donald E. *1959–60* Music
Barrett, Nathan *1965–66* Playwriting
Barrutia, Richard *1962–63* Spanish
Bass, Floyd L. *1957–58* Education
Bass, George H. *1963–64* Drama
Batista, Jorge *1964–65* Sociology
Batson, Susan A. *1965–66* Acting
Battle, Joseph *1961–62* Mathematics
Bell, C. H. *1963–64* Music Composition
Bell, Wendolyn Y. *1961–62* Romance Lang.
Benally, Nancy *1958–60* Biology
Benavidez, Edward F. *1971–72* Sociol.
Bencomo, Rose E. *1971–72* Sociology
Benson, Gloria J. *1967–68* Mathematics
Berry, Lee Roy, Jr. *1970–71* Government
Bess, William C. *1970–71* History
Blackburn, R. H. *1952–53* Graphic Arts
Blackwell, James E. *1958–59* Sociology
Blair, Thelma Lee *1953–54* Public Admin.
Blair, Thomas L. *1953–54* Sociology
Blake, J. Herman *1963–64* Sociology
Blatchford, Herbert C. *1958–59* Law
Blount, Joyce A. *1970–71* Education
Bobonis, Idalia C. *1964–65* Spanish Lit.
Bolden, Theodore E. *1951–52* Dentistry
Bonafoux, Fernando *1962–63* Anesthesia
Bonilla, Frank *1954–55* Sociology
Bormanshinov, Arash *1956–57* Philology
Borridge, John Jr. *1954–55* Law
Boyd, Joseph F., Jr. *1956–57* Medicine
Bradshaw, Alice *1962–63* Social Work
Braswell, Bruce K. *1960–61* Philosophy

*Women's married names in parentheses.

183

Brau, Maria Milagros *1956–57* Humanities
Brawner, Alpha L. *1961–62* Voice
Brean, David Z. *1956–57* Painting
Brimmer, Andrew F. *1950–51* Economics
Brown, Debria *1959–60* Voice
Brown, Frank London *1958–59* Literature
Brown, Letitia Woods *1953–54* History
Brown, M. E. (Turner) *1965–66* Human Relat.
Brown, Paul L. *1953–54* Zoology
Browne, Dallas L. *1971–72* Anthropol.
Browne, F. D., II *1959–60* Mech. Eng.
Bryant, Betty H. *1970–71* Education
Bumbry, Grace A. *1958–59* Voice
Buncombe, Marie H. *1960–61* English
Burbridge, E. D., Jr. *1965–66* Scenic Design
Burchard, Gloria Gonzalez *1955–56* Hist.
Burkett, William T. *1967–68* Social Work
Burks, Matthew *1952–53* Psychology
Burrell, Theodore A. *1969–70* Law
Burton, Miriam E. *1955–56* Voice
Bustamante, John H. *1952–53* Law
Butcher, Philip *1951–52* English
Butler, Berthea L. *1967–68* Guidance
Butler, Hilda L. *1965–66* Business Educ.
Bynoe, James A. *1963–64* Painting
Byrd, Carol (Anderson) *1965–66* Economics
Cabrera, Edna E. *1971–72* Medicine
Cachu, Mary L. *1968–69* Education
Cadena, Carlos C. *1951–52* Law
Cahn, Jean Camper *1960–61* Law
Campbell, Johnny, Jr. *1964–65* Int. Affairs
Campbell, Lorenzo M. *1967–68* Sociology
Canino, Maria J. *1965–66* Social Work
Cantero, Catalino L. *1970–71* Social Work
Capello, Juan J. *1965–66* Medicine
Caples, Edgar Lee *1970–71* Elect. Eng.
Carey, Thomas *1959–60* Voice
Carney, Carmen *1971–72* Spanish Lit.
Carro, John *1955–56* Law
Carroll, Constance M. *1967–68* Classics
Carruthers, Benito *1963–64* Acting
Carter, George N. *1964–65* Political Sci.
Carter, Yvonne *1954–55* Law
Casada, James Allen *1971–72* History
Casillas, Enrique F. *1969–70* Dentistry
Cassadore, P. A. *1959–60* Law Apprentice
Castillo, Daniel T. *1970–71* Law
Castillo, Peter G., Jr. *1971–72* History
Caswell, James O. *1962–63* Art History
Cata, Juanita O. *1968–69* Education
Cazares, Roy B. *1971–72* Law
Chambers, Julius L. *1961–62* Law
Chambers, Yolande H. *1952–53* Law
Chang, Diana *1954–55* Literature
Chang, Thomas M. C. *1956–57* Psychology
Chang, Yi-an *1956–57* Piano
Chase, B. (Ribaud) *1957–58* Sculpture, Graphics
Chavez, Antonio E. *1971–72* Education
Chen, Barbara *1960–61* Medicine
Chen, David Y. *1961–62* Asian Studies
Cherot, Romeo A. *1950–51* Political Sci.
Ching, Doris C. *1957–58* Education
Chinn, Y. Y. *1956–57* Painting
Chino, Frederic H. *1953–54* Sociology

Chong, Kenneth D. *1960–61* Law
Christian, Alphonso A. *1966–67* Law
Christian, Cora L. *1968–69* Medicine
Christopher, James E. *1954–55* Geology
Chuan, Marian *1956–57* Social Work
Chuculate, R. W. *1956–57* Social Work
Chung, Stanley M. K. *1958–59* Medicine
Church, Robert L. *1964–65* Medicine
Clark, Arcola E. *1964–65* Music Educ.
Clark, Betty L. (Wilson) *1957–58* Nursing
Clark, Charles A. *1959–60* Dentistry
Clark, Edgar R. *1953–54* Music Comp.
Clark, James N. *1963–64* Dentistry
Clarke, Frank *1950–51* Medicine
Clarke, Jacquelyne *1959–60* Sociology
Clay, Eric L. *1969–70* Law
Clendeninn, Neil J. *1971–72* Medicine
Clifton, Fred J. *1960–61* Philosophy
Coard, Robert M. *1964–65* City Planning
Colbert, Helen *1951–52* Voice
Coleman, Ernest *1963–64* Physics
Coleman, Peter Tali *1950–51* Law
Collins, Alma C. *1951–52* French
Colon, Fernando *1962–63* Psychology
Condelaro, Richard *1950–51* Hosp. Admin.
Conwell, Kathleen A. *1965–66* French
Cook, Mercer *1952–53* Political Sci.
Cook, Samuel D. *1952–53* Political Sci.
Cooke, Wilhelmina *1970–71* Law
Cordova, Edward *1964–65* Amer. Studies
Cordova, Gilbert B. *1967–68* History
Cordova, Juanito *1958–59* Social Work
Corona, Maria L. *1971–72* Social Work
Cortes, Ramiro *1960–61* Music Comp.
Corwin, Mary DeOca *1966–67* Anthropology
Courtwright, V. T. *1956–57* Social Work
Cowans, Adger W. *1963–64* Photography
Cramer, Joe J. *1959–60* Business Admin.
Crenshaw, Audrey E. *1968–69* Nursing
Crosby, J. H., Jr. *1960–61* Social Work
Cross, Jereldine (Redcorn) *1962–63* Mathematics
Cross, Raymond *1970–71* Law
Crump, Iris *1963–64* Painting
Cruz, Antonio R. *1967–68* Public Admin.
Cruz, Emilio A. *1964–65* Painting
Cullers, Samuel J. *1950–52* City Planning
Curl, Charles H., Jr. *1970–71* Law
Curtis, Nancy C. *1959–60 1961–62* Educ.
Dalton, Margaret D. (Setchkarev) *1959–60* Slavic Lit.
Daniel, Billie Lynn *1961–62* Voice
Daniel, G. B., Jr. *1954–55* Romance Lang.
Daniels, Douglas H. *1971–72* History
Danner, Margaret *1959–60* Poetry
Dash, Calvin O. *1951–52* Music
Davids, Dorothy W. *1963–64* Social Sci.
Davila, Jose D. *1953–55* Social Work
Davis, Elaine C. *1957–58* Education
Davis, George A. *1958–59* Business Admin.
Davis, N. F. *1957–58* Economics
Day, Wynona Gunter *1959–60* Social Work
De Aguero, Arthur *1967–68* Art Education
DeGarmo, Elivinia R. *1969–70* Social Work
de Jongh, John P. *1952–54* Law

Gwaltney, John L. *1961–62* Anthropol.
Gwynn, Donald G. *1960–61* Painting
Hamilton, Charles V. *1962–63* Polit. Sci.
Hamilton, Stephen G. *1963–64* Physics
Hammock, John C. *1970–71* Law
Han, Raymond Gung Jah *1961–62* Painting
Harcum, C. A. *1967–68* Lat. American Studies
Harding, Vincent G. *1952–53* Journalism
Harris, G. S., Jr. *1954–55* Painting
Harris, Hollon L. *1952–53* Fine Arts
Harris, J. T., Jr. *1952–53* Public Admin.
Harrison, Sandas L. *1961–62* History
Harvey, Geraldine D. *1951–52* Education
Hata, Y. (Mukai) *1956–57* Social Work
Hatch, John W. *1964–65* Law
Hawkins, Eugene R. *1965–66* Painting
Hawkins, Valerie R. (Boulware) *1969–70* Anthropol.
Hayashi, Kaname *1956–57* Painting
Hayashida, Frank *1958–59* Education
Haynes, Ulric St. C., Jr. *1953–54* Law
Hearn, Robert W. *1965–66* Political Sci.
Hecker-Grade, Inna *1955–56* Russian, Comp. Lit.
Hector, Dorene E. *1969–70* Linguistics
Heine, Dwight *1958–59* Education
Hemachandra, Neal *1953–54* Music Educ.
Henry, Bethwel *1958–59* Public Admin.
Henry, Ragan A. *1959–60* Law
Heras, Ivonne *1971–72* Clin. Psychol.
Hernandez, Abimael *1958–59, 1961–62* Political Science
Hernandez, Susan *1968–69* Spanish Lit.
Herndon, Arthur L. *1961–62* Voice
Hidalgo, Elia (Christensen) *1956–58* Psychol.
Hidalgo, Jesus F. *1969–70* Lat. Amer. Hist.
Higginbotham, A. Leon, Jr. *1952–53* Law
High, Carl E. *1961–62* Business Admin.
Hillaire, Mary E. *1964–65* Education
Hinderas, N. L. (Monagas) *1950–51* Piano
Hinton, Albert L. *1964–65* English
Hirabayashi, James A. *1957–58* Anthropol.
Hirakawa, M. O. (Myers) *1954–55* Guidance
Hobbs, Gloria L. *1957–58* Romance Lang.
Hobbs, Orlando S. *1951–52* Law
Hogan, Lloyd L. *1951–52* Economics
Holliman, Philip D. ...*1957–58* Social Work
Holman, M. C. *1950–51, 1952–53* Writing
Holmes, E. K. (Norton) *1961–62* Law
Holmes, R. A. *1967–69* Internat. Relations
Hong, Arabella *1956–57* Voice
Hood, Robert E. *1962–63* Philos., Relig.
Hood, Rodney G. *1971–72* Medicine
Hoover, Dorothy E. *1954–55* Mathematics
Horiuchi, Russell N. *1954–55* Polit. Sci.
Hornback, May Shiga *1957–58* Nursing
Horne, Theodore R., Jr. *1959–60* Law
Houston, A. (Hopson) *1966–67* Math.
Houston, Earline L. *1964–65* Medicine
Huang, Alice S. *1960–61* Medicine
Huerta, John E. *1966–68* Law
Huggins, Kathryn *1955–56* Anthropology
Huggins, Nathan I. *1955–56, 1959–60* History

Hughes, Joyce Ann *1962–63* Law
Hunsberger, Martin S., Jr. *1953–54* Social Work
Hunter, Bernard, Jr. *1956–57* Music Educ.
Hunter, K. E. (Lattany) *1959–60* Writing
Ibanez, Alfonso *1971–72* Law
Ibanez, Grace K. *1970–71* Education
Idar, Ed, Jr. *1954–56* Law
Iglesias, Josefina *1960–61* Philosophy
Ignace, Gerald L. *1963–64* Medicine
Illanes, Fernando *1964–65* Voice
Inamoto, Noboru *1953–54* Public Law, Govt.
Inoway, Carl *1962–63* Architecture
Iriarte, L. L. G. *1955–56* Pub. Health
Irikura, James K. *1955–56* Asian History
Isaac, Calvin J. *1967–68* Education
Iseri, Oscar A. *1953–54* Medicine
Ito, Miyoko (Ichiyasu) *1951–52* Painting
Ivory, Delores L. *1964–65* Voice
Iwamoto, Ralph S. *1958–59* Painting
Izcoa, Ada E. *1962–63* Clinical Psychol.
Izquierdo, Domingo, Jr. *1959–60* Painting
Jackson, Clarence B. *1963–64* Music
Jackson, Clifford E. *1957–58* Painting
Jackson, Esther M. *1956–57* Speech, Drama
Jackson, Henry F. *1966–67* Political Sci.
Jackson, Kennell A., Jr. *1963–64* African Studies
Jackson, Raymond T. *1963–64* Piano
Jackson, Rhea *1954–55* Voice
Jacobo, Paulina M. *1971–72* Law
Jacques, Felix A. *1957–58* Biology
James, Luther *1959–60* Drama
James, M. Lucia *1959–60* Education
Jeanpierre, W. A. *1962–63* Modern Lang.
Jeffries, L., Jr. *1964–66* Law, Govt.
Jenkins, J. H., Jr. *1950–51* Amer. Studies
Jenkins, Lee C. *1964–65* Theater Hist.
Jenkins, Thomas H. *1960–61* City Planning
Jennings, H. T. *1967–68* Int. Relations
Joe, Dale Gordon *1953–54* Painting
Johnson, Albert J. *1960–61* Theater Arts
Johnson, Benjamin T. *1952–53* Translating
Johnson, Carl L. *1955–56* Oral Surgery
Johnson, Daniel L. *1963–64* Painting
Johnson, Ford T., Jr. *1965–66* Law
Johnson, Iris M. *1964–65* Oriental & African Studies
Johnson, James R. *1950–51* Medicine
Johnson, Marcella *1971–72* Social Work
Johnson, Mary Ray *1953–55* Medicine
Johnson, Thomas W. *1959–60* Medicine
Johnson, Tobe *1959–60* Political Sci.
Johnson, Willard R. *1962–63* Polit. Sci.
Jones, George T. *1951–52, 1953–54* Philosophy
Jones, James A. *1954–55* Sociology
Jones, James E., Jr. *1953–55* Law
Jones, Louis C. *1958–59* Law
Jones, Marva Paulette *1967–68* Law
Jorrin, Mario *1961–62* Photography
Juarez, Jose R. *1961–62* Lat. Amer. Studies
Kapitz, Donald R. *1969–70* Social Work
Katsuizumi, Anne (Chew) *1951–52*

Social Work
Kee, Brenda E. _1968–69_ Music Education
Keene, Paul F. _1951–52_ Painting
Keith, Laurel E. _1955–56_ Medicine
Keith, Shirley _1964–65_ Anthropology
Kelley, William M., Jr. _1963–64_ Writing
Kellman, Denis E. _1970–71_ Law
Kempler, Bernhard _1958–59_ Psychology
Kendall, Wilfred I. _1962–63_ Pub. Admin.
Killebrew, Gwendolyn _1965–66_ Voice
Kilson, Martin L. _1955–56_ Political Sci.
Kim, L. (Joseph) _1958–59_ Law
Kim, Stanley _1955–56_ Social Work
Kimbrough, Marvin G. _1965–66_
  Linguistics
King, Irving M. _1955–56_ Law
King, Juanita _1963–64_ Voice
King, Patricia A. _1967–68_ Law
King, Woodie, Jr. _1965–66_ Theater
Kinney, Rubellite (Johnson) _1954–55_
  Folklore
Kirkwood, James I. _1960–61_ Soil Science
Kitagawa, Masa _1955–56_ Piano
Kitaguchi, I. (Nishimura) _1960–61_
  Social Stud.
Kitsuse, John I. _1951–53_ Sociology
Knight, Yvonne T. _1965–66_ Education
Kobayashi, Robert H. _1958–59_ Painting
Kosinski, Tatiana _1958–59_ Slavic Lang.
Kumagai, Lindy F. _1952–53_ Medicine
Kumekawa, Ryozo G. _1954–55_ Sociology
Kyles, I. M. (Jeter) _1969–70_ Audiology
Labat, Alvin V. _1953–54_ French, Linguist.
Ladd, Edmund J. _1955–57_ Anthropology
Lafayette, Leonora G. _1950–51_ Voice
LaPointe, Eric J. _1970–71_ Guidance
La Pointe, Francis C. _1966–67_ Journalism
Larsen, Jean D. _1962–63_ Physics
Laster, Georgia A. _1953–54_ Voice
Lastra-Gonzalez, Carlos J. _1956–57_
  Economics
Latimer, James H. _1962–63_ Music
Lattimore, Emerson A. _1963–64_ Chemistry
Lavandero, C. F. _1960–61_ City Planning
Lavigne, M. E., Jr. _1967–68_ Engineering
Leak, John C., Jr. _1951–52_ Chemistry
Lee, Charles B. _1950–51_ Zoology
Lee, Gary _1950–51_ History
Lee, Murrel David _1970–71_ Architecture
Lee, Thelma (Blair) _1953–54_
  Public Admin.
Lemelle, Adeline (Evans) _1961–62_
  Speech Therapy
LeMelle, T. J. _1964–65_ Int. Relations
Leong, James C. _1953–54_ Painting
Levita, Eric _1956–57_ Clinical Psychol.
Lewis, Diane K. (Chaney) _1955–56_
  Anthropol.
Lewis, Edwin E. _1955–56_ Painting
Lewis, J. E. (Madabunyi) _1965–66_
  Social Work
Lewis, Moses R. _1963–64_ African Studies
Levy, Fernando J. _1966–67_ Language, Lit.
Lima, Frank _1964–65_ Poetry
Lincoln, C. Eric _1957–59_ Human Relations
Lindsey, Claudia _1965–66_ Voice
Lindsey, Gloria C. _1970–71_ Sociology
Lockley, Jeanette _1957–58_ Mathematics

Loloma, Charles _1951–52_ Ceramics
Lombard, Rudolph J. _1964–65_ Social Sci.
Lopez, Minerva G. _1968–69_ English
Louie, Richard _1960–61_ Far East Studies
Lowe, Mary J. _1954–56_ Law
Lowry, James H. _1963–64_ Public Admin.
Lucero, Ernest _1960–61_ Geography
Lucero, John A. _1971–72_ Physics
Lucero, Joseph A. _1968–69_ Social Work
Lucero, Joe I. _1956–58_ Medicine
Ludley, A. M. (Finley) _1957–58_ Sociol.
Lujan, James _1970–71_ Guidance
MacDonald, Lonnie, N. _1958–59_
  Psychiatry
Machado, Manuel A., Jr. _1962–63_
  Latin American Hist.
Macias, Gloria _1964–65_ Spanish Lit.
Madison, Eugene W. _1963–64_ Mathematics
Maestas, Gilbert B. _1950–52_ Medicine
Magassy, K. J. _1956–57_ Slavic Lang., Lit.
Majors, William _1960–61_ Painting
Maldonado, D. C. _1970–71_ Polit. Theory
Maldonado-Denis M. _1957–58_ Polit. Sci.
Mallory, E. (Smith) _1955–56_ Social Work
Mangefel, John Avila _1956–57_ Education
Manicur, Alice R. _1958–60_ Education
Manuel, C. J. _1963–64_ Apprentice, Law
Marquez, Mary N. _1956–57_ Nursing
Marshall, Gloria A. _1959–60_ Anthropol.
Marshall, K. E. _1957–58_ Social Work
Martinez, Arthur D. _1970–71_ Polit. Sci.
Martinez, John R. _1955–56_ History
Martinez, Jose A. _1966–67_ Economics
Martinez, Phillip U. _1954–56_ Medicine
Martinez, Quino E. _1952–53_
  Romance Lang.
Martinez, Vilma S. (Singer) _1964–65_ Law
Mason, Charles _1958–59_ Reading
Massel, Gregory J. _1954–55_ Polit. Sci.
Matsumoto, Yoshiharu _1955–56_ Sociology,
  Anthropology
Mayhew, Richard _1958–59_ Painting
Maynor, H. M. (Schierbeck) _1957–58_
  Govt.
McAdory, John T. _1970–71_ Medicine
McCoy, Elaine _1960–61_ Business Educ.
McDonald, Alonzo E. _1956–57_ Dentistry
McDougall, Harold A., III _1969–70_ Law
McKay, Iliff _1951–52_ Business Admin.
McKinney, Ernest R. _1964–65_ Polit. Sci.
McMechen, Mary J. _1952–53_ Voice
McPherson, Ruth _1957–58_ Int. Relations
Meares, Cecil H., Jr. _1952–53_ Medicine
Medicine, Beatrice G. _1952–53_ Anthropol.
Meeks, Thomas O., Jr. _1954–55_ Physics
Meyers, Ishmael _1962–63_ Business Admin.
Middleton, Samuel M. _1959–60_ Painting
Mihaly, Zoltan M. _1958–59_ Law
Miles, Elijah W. _1961–62_ Government
Miller, Joan _1960–61_ Dance Education
Miller, Samson _1956–57_ Forestry
Milner, Ronald S. _1962–63_ Writing
Mindiola, Tatcho, Jr. _1970–71_ Sociology
Miranda, Magdalena _1963–64_ Social Work
Mireles, Sylvester R. _1960–61_ Zoology
Mitchell, Daniel B. _1963–64_ Polit. Sci.
Mitchell, Joseph D. _1971–72_ Law
Mitchell, Joyce (Cook) _1956–57_ Philos.

Mitchell, Marilyn *1964–65* Political Sci.
Miyasaki, George J. *1957–58* Fine Arts
Momaday, N. Scott *1962–63* Amer. Lit.
Monteith, James D. *1957–58* Law
Montoya, Rebecca *1958–59* Social Work
Montoya, Velma (Thompson) *1959–60* Law
Moore, Roy N. *1951–52* Painting
Mootry, Maria *1966–67* English Lit.
Mora, Raul E. *1969–70* Law
Morales, Julio, Jr. *1966–67* Social Work
Moreno, Steve G. *1965–67* Guidance
Morgan, Norma *1951–52* Painting
Morris, Joseph B. *1955–56* Chemistry
Morrison, George *1953–54* Painting
Moses, Paul B. *1963–65* Art Hist.
Moses, Robert P. *1956–57* Philosophy
Moses, Resio S. *1969–70* Public Admin.
Mosley, Robert, Jr. *1962–63* Voice
Moss, Edith C. *1967–68* Romance Lang.
Motofuji, Frank T. *1954–55* Japanese Lit.
Moy, Seong *1950–51* Painting
Munoz, Rogelio *1971–72* Law
Murrah, William A., Jr. *1968–69* Sociol. Psychiatry of Religion
Nakai, Lillian Y. (Campbell) *1959–60* Area Studies
Nakai, Thomas *1961–62* Dentistry
Nakamura, Mamoru *1966–67* Law
Nava, Julian *1951–52, 1953–54* Polit. Sci.
Navarro, Richard A. *1969–70* Dentistry
Neal, Betty J. *1965–66* Statistics
Neal, Homer A., Jr. *1961–62* Physics
Neal, Nana *1970–71* Education
Neely, George, Jr. *1959–60* Physics
Nelson, David J., Jr. *1967–68* Psychology
Newton, Dolores *1961–62* Anthropology
Ng, David *1958–59* Theology
Ngiraklsong, Arthur *1967–68* Polit. Sci.
Nicks, Walter B. *1956–57* Dance
Nieves, Josephine *1962–63* Social Work
Nishi, Setsuko *1950–51* Sociology
Niyekawa, Agnes (Howard) *1958–59* Psychology
Norman, Memphis *1964–65* Sociology
Norton, Dolores G. *1966–67* Social Work
Obet, Heli *1955–56* Dentistry
Ochikubo, Tetsuo *1957–58* Painting
Oden, Gloria C. *1955–57* Poetry
O'Donnell, Pat D. *1968–69* Medicine
Okada, Frank *1957–58* Painting
Okimoto, Jerry T. *1955–56* Painting
Olivarez, Grace *1968–70* Law
Oliver, George B. *1954–56* English Lit.
Oliver, James *1971–72* Medicine
Olives, Michael *1969–70* Dentistry
Olivo, Efren *1961–62* Medicine
One Feather, Gerald *1960–61* Government
Ortiz, A. *1961–62, 1964–65* Anthropol.
Ortiz, Filemon, Jr. *1970–71* Law
Ortiz, Ralph *1965–66* Art Education
Pabon, Milton *1960–61* Polit. Sci.
Padilla, F. V. *1970–71* Polit. Sci.
Padilla, Mary S. *1971–72* City Planning
Padilla, S. L. *1969–70, 1971–72* Medicine
Padoch, Jaroslaw *1955–56* Law
Palmer, Larry I. *1968–69* Law
Palmer, R. *1956–57* Internat. Affairs

Pangelinan, Adriano *1961–62* Painting
Pantoja, Antonia *1953–54* Social Work
Partida, San Juanita *1970–71* Spanish
Patridge, Melvin *1961–62* Writing
Patton, B. (Miller) *1962–63* Dance
Payne, Charles B., Jr. *1961–62* Medicine
Pedraza, A. E. *1971–72* Health Educ.
Pemberton, Ruth Naomi *1967–68* Social Work
Pena, Lionel Aron *1959–60* Law
Peratrovich, Roy *1952–53* Finance
Perea, Richard A. *1970–71* Polit. Sci.
Perez, Gerald J. *1968–69* Wildlife Mgt.
Perez, Rita L. *1967–68* Comparative Lit.
Pointer, Edwin L. *1953–55* Medicine
Pomare, Eleo *1961–62* Dance
Porter, Jonnie (Hamilton) *1960–61* Zoology
Powell, Philip M. *1967–68* Psychology
Pugh, Paula L. *1971–72* Law
Puig, Hector *1959–60* Psychology
Puryear, Alvin *1960–61* Business Admin.
Pressley, L. (Lazaruk) *1951–52* Guidance
Prince, Dorothy Mae *1961–62* Education
Quetone, Allen *1958–59* Law
Quevedo, J. B. *1970–71* Spanish Lang., Lit.
Ra, Jong Wook *1963–65* Government
Raigoza, James *1961–62* Medical Sociol.
Rainer, Ann P. *1966–67* Anthropology
Rainer, John C. *1951–52* Education
Ramarui, David *1957–58* Anthropology
Ramsey, Henry, Jr. *1962–63* Law
Ramsey, Vivian Scott *1952–53* Piano
Randall, H. E., Jr. *1964–65* Photography
Randolph, T. H., Jr. *1969–70* Social Work
Rawlings, Howard P. *1959–60* Mathematics
Redwolf, Rosella *1969–70* Guidance
Reifel, Albert D. *1950–51* Medicine
Reifel, Benjamin *1951–52* Agricultural Economics, Government
Reifel, Pakali *1954–55* Social Work
Render, Frank W., II *1966–67* Journalism, Mass Communication
Reyes, David *1971–72* Law
Reynold, Pearl A. (Grice) *1964–65* Dance
Reynolds, Ruthie G. *1968–69* Bus. Admin.
Rhoades, Everett R. *1954–56* Medicine
Ridgel, Gus *1952–53* Labor Economics
Ridgley, James O. *1970–71* Medicine
Riley, Sam *1958–59* Human Relations
Rios, Albert J. *1951–52* Biology
Rivers, Haywood *1952–53* Fine Arts
Rivers, Louis, Jr. *1957–58* Theater
Roach, Hildred *1960–61* Music Education
Robbs, Mary E. *1953–54* Voice
Roberts, Thomas L. *1964–65* Microbiology
Robinson, David J. *1961–63* Law
Robinson, James *1964–65* Law
Robinson, Joan E. *1971–72* Law
Robinson, William A., Jr. *1951–52* Writing
Rodgers, Rod *1965–66* Dance
Rodriguez, Ramon *1966–67* City Planning
Rogers, Nannie *1963–64* Guidance
Rogosin, Boris Ivan *1957–58* History

Rollins, Esther (McIntosh) 1952–53 Pychology
Rolls, James 1960–61 Biology
Romano, Octavio 1954–56 Anthropol.
Rosario, Ramon 1953–54 Photography
Rose, Harold M. 1957–58 Geography
Rose, John T. 1969–70 Law
Ross, Dorothy (Dash) 1952–53 Voice
Ross, Hubert B. 1951–52 Anthropology
Ross, S. E. (Talbot) 1956–57 Publ. Hlth.
Rout, Leslie B., Jr. 1964–65 History
Rozek, Edward J. 1953–54 Political Sci.
Rucker, Henry L. 1967–68 Law
Ruiz, Chris C. 1962–63 Social Work
Ruiz, Ramon E. 1950–51 History
Rumph, Judy Ann 1968–69 Speech Pathol.
Rush, Sheila (Jones) 1963–64 Law
Rushing, Jack D. 1966–67 Law
Russell, Marian 1955–56 English
Salas, G. Ricardo 1957–58 Law
Samora, Julian 1950–52 Anthropology
Samuels, Linda R. (McKinnon) 1951–52 Sociology
Sanchez, Jose M. 1971–72 Polit. Sci.
Sanchez, Pedro Cruz 1950–52 Educ.
Sanchez, Raymond 1970–71 Medicine
Sanchez, Willie 1961–62 Education
Sanchez, Yolanda 1964–65 Social Work
Sandbergen, Konto 1953–54 Public Admin.
Sanders, Earl A. 1964–65 Music Educ.
Sanders, Rita 1965–66 History
Sandoval, A. David 1963–64 Economics
Santiago, Anthony 1957–58 Social Work
Santiago, Ramon L. 1962–63 Education
Santiago, Ruben E. 1959–61 Anthropol.
Sarosi, George A. 1962–63 Medicine
Sato, Tadashi 1954–55 Painting
Sawyer, Laura 1962–63 Law
Scholder, Fritz 1962–63 Painting
Scott, Charlotte H. (Nathan) 1960–61 Economics
Scott, Joseph W. 1960–61 Sociology
Scott, Kathleen J. 1966–67 Nursing
Scruggs, Otey 1955–56 History
Seda-Bonilla, Edwin 1953–55 Sociol.
Segundo, Thomas A. 1954–56 Social Sci.
Seki, Hoken S. 1962–63 Law
Seneca, M. E., Jr. 1967–68 Publ. Admin.
Shibuya, Manabu (McDonald) 1957–58 Social Work
Shinoda, Minoru 1951–52 History
Shiraishi, U. (Dwyer) 1957–58 Social Work
Shores, William R., Jr. 1965–66 Voice
Shropshire, C. N., Jr. 1953–55 Medicine
Siales, Ermes 1961–62 Polit. Devel.
Silbajoris, Frank 1953–55 Russian Lit.
Simms, Gregory 1954–55 Voice
Singer, Jerome 1953–54 Mining Eng.
Singleton, Robert 1963–64 Economics
Sinkler, George 1958–59 Education
Skinner, Elliott P. 1953–54 Anthropol.
Smith, Bill Ray Dotson 1970–71 Italian
Smith, Robert Peter, Jr. 1958–59 French
Smothers, Curtis R. 1964–65 Law
Sneed, Woodrow B. 1963–64 Law
Snowden, B. C. (Donahue) 1961–62

American Lit.
Solang, Mitsuo 1965–66 Sociology
Soto, Maria (Humberto) 1950–51 Nursing
Spang, Alonzo T., Sr. 1961–62 Guidance
Spearman, Rawn 1951–52 Voice
Spratlen, Thaddeus H. 1958–59 Economics
Springer, A. M. 1965–66 Social Work
Spruce, Beryl 1961–62 Medicine
Spurlock, Karla J. 1971–72 Amer. Studies
Stafford, Douglas 1955–56 Education
Stallworth, B. E. 1967–68 Social Work
Stambuk, George 1956–57 Polit. Sci.
Stancell, A. F. 1959–60 Chemical Eng.
Stanford, Carolyn (Fortson) 1958–59 Voice
Stanley, Maxine 1971–72 English Lit.
Starks, B. (Favazza) 1962–63 Medicine
Steele, Lois Fister 1962–63 Zoology
Sterling, Eleonore 1951–52 History
Stern, Paul J. 1954–55 Psychology
Stevens, Betty (Walker) 1964–66 Law
Stewart, J. T., Jr. 1952–54 Transport.
Stewart, Sandra A. 1971–72 Social Work
Stoakley, Zlmarian J. 1966–67 Sociology
Stratmon, David 1954–55 Polit. Sci.
Suarez, Mario 1957–58 Writing
Suda, Frances K. 1953–54 History
Sugimoto, Albert H. 1958–59 Painting
Sullivan, H. (Challenor) 1963–64 Polit. Sci.
Sullivan, Louis W. 1960–61 Medicine
Summers, Barbara 1967–68 French Lit.
Sunada, Kayo 1958–59 Medicine
Sunia, Fofo 1959–61 Economics
Suzuki, James H. 1958–59 Painting
Suzuki, Peter 1954–55 Anthropology
Swift, John A. 1965–66 Voice
Swan, Robert J. 1971–72 Guidance
Swing, Thomas K. 1958–59 Law
Szabo, George 1961–62 Hist. of Art
Tajiri, Shinkichi 1960–61 Sculpture
Takechi, Dorothy K. (Tada) 1952–53 Human Relations
Talamantes, F. J., Jr. 1970–71 Endocrinol.
Tanikawa, Frances 1960–61 History
Tarkong, John S. 1965–66 Law
Tate, Harry Terrell 1971–72 Medicine
Tate, James D. 1971–72 Medicine
Taylor, C. W., Jr. 1958–59 Anthropol.
Taylor, Leonard 1962–63 Photography
Taylor Orlando L. 1962–63 Speech Pathology, Audiology
Terasaki, George K. 1964–65 Painting
Testa, Mayda 1965–66 Voice
Thomas, Earl P. 1964–65 Social Work
Thomas, James A. 1963–64 Law
Thomas, Robert K. 1953–54 Anthropology
Thompson, Robert L. 1962–63 Painting
Thompson, S. 1961–63 City Planning
Thornell, Richard 1956–57 Publ. Affairs
Thornton, Marilyn 1957–58 Drama
Thurston, Maxine A. 1963–64 Social Work
Tinnin, Alvis Lee 1955–57 French Lit.
Tokuyama, George H. 1955–56 Publ. Hlth.
Tolbert, Bruce Edward 1971–72 Law
Tolbert, Henry 1971–72 Linguistics
Tolbert, Herman A. 1970–71 Medicine

Tollett, Charles A. 1956–57 Medicine
Tolson, Melvin B., Jr. 1959–60 French
Tong, Te-kong 1956–57 American History
Toppin, Edgar A. 1953–54 History
Toribiong, Johnson 1971–72 Law
Torres, Blanca 1969–70 Social Work
Torres, Joseph B. 1952–53 Social Work
Townsend, R. S. 1964–65 Playwriting
Townsley, Humphrey 1960–61 Medicine
Trimillos, R. 1965–66 Ethnomusicology
Trotty, Thelie 1957–58 Social Studies
Truitte, James F. 1959–60 Dance
Trujillo, George N. 1956–57 Social Work
Trujillo, Michael H. 1969–71 Medicine
Tsai, Wen-Ying 1963–64 Painting
Tsien, Elaine 1960–61 Medicine
Tsuchidana, Harry S. 1959–60 Painting
Tsuneishi, Warren M. 1954–55 Polit. Sci.
Turner, James E. 1966–67 African Studies
Twine, Edgar H. 1957–58 Law
Two Hawk, Webster A. 1956–57 Religion
Twyman, Electa 1963–64 Drama
Tyler, Veronica 1962–63 Voice
Uemura, Joseph N. 1957–58 Philosophy
Underwood, Robert A. 1971–72 History
Utu, Falefatu S. 1958–59 Government
Uyeki, Eugene S. 1951–52 Sociology
Valdez, Abelardo L. 1970–71 Law
Valdez, Emilia 1970–71 Nursing
Valencia, Richard R. 1970–71 Guidance
Valentine, M. D. 1969–70 African Studies
Valle, Marta 1956–57, 1960–61 Social
  Work
Valtin, Heinz 1952–53 Medicine
Van Buren, Harvey, Jr. 1956–57 Piano
Van Brunt, Constance W. 1971–72 Educ.
Varela, Delfino 1950–52 Social Work
Vargas, Philip G. 1961–62 Sociology
Vault, W. L. 1957–58 Physics, Math.
Vazquez, Alida 1960–61 Dance Therapy
Vega, Anthony M. 1971–72 Sociology
Vega, Rafael 1961–62 Social Work
Velez, Ramon 1966–67 Medicine
Venegas, Moises 1964–65 History
Verrett, Shirley (Lomonaco) 1957–58
  Voice
Vigil, Ralph H. 1959–60 History
Villareal, Albert 1966–68 Romance Lang.
Vincent, Ubert C. 1954–55 Psychology
Vigil, Joseph 1952–53 Medicine
Wachsler, L. (Haberman) 1955–56 Classics
Walker, George 1971–72 Amer. Hist.
Walker, George T. 1958–59 Music
Walker, John W. 1960–61 Sociology
Wallace, Fred 1962–63 Law
Wallace, Walter 1959–61 Sociology
Walters, Gwendolyn A. 1961–62 Voice
Ward, Haskell 1965–66 Sociology
Ward, John P. 1955–56 Polit. Sci.
Warrior, Clyde M. 1967–68 Sociology
Warren, Dave 1959–60 History
Waters, James L. 1967–68 Economics
Watkins, Charles 1964–65 English Lit.
Watt, Melvin L. 1968–69 Law

Weakley, Floyd L. 1963–64 Mathematics
Weaver, Harold 1962–63 Area Studies
Weaver, Thomas 1962–63 Anthropology
Weil, R. L., Jr. 1961–62 Sculpture
Weital, Daro 1962–63 Education
West, Lucretia 1951–52 Voice
West, Walter R., Jr. 1968–69 Law
White, Andrew N., III 1964–65 Oboe
White, Carl D. 1955–56 Voice
White, Charles W. 1955–56 Painting
White, Dennis R. 1969–70 Mathematics
White, Eugene A. 1962–63 Medicine
White, Jacqueline 1958–59 Education
White, Joseph S., Jr. 1963–64 Writing
White, Willie 1957–58 Theology, Philos.
Whitfield, Marcus H., Jr. 1963–64 Math.
Whitten, Jacky 1964–65 Painting
Wiley, George A. 1955–56 Chemistry
Wiggins, Bernard A. 1968–69 Medicine
Wilks, Danny Ray 1971–72 Medicine
Willerford, Frederick 1952–53 Russian
Williams, Edna 1959–60 Voice
Williams, Elmyra 1970–71 French
Williams, Henry L., Jr. 1969–70 Accting.
Williams, Walter H. 1955–56 Painting
Williams, Todd 1965–66 Sculpt.
Williamson, Mary (McHenry) 1954–55,
  1957–58 American Literature
Willis, John R., Jr. 1961–62 History
Willis, William S., Jr. 1950–51 Anthropol.
Wills, J. N., Jr. 1968–69 Urban Planning
Wilson, C. Z., Jr. 1955–56 Economics
Wilson, John 1950–51 Painting
Wilson, Ricardo A. 1969–70 Medicine
Wilson, Robert J. 1960–61 Voice
Wilson, Warren G. 1960–61 Piano
Winston, Michael 1966–67 History
Wise, James F. 1958–59 History of Art
Wise, Milton Bee 1950–51 Agriculture
Woo, Gary 1956–57 Painting
Wood, Marie 1954–55 History
Wright, J. A. (Jackson) 1964–65 Social
  Work
Wright, Marian (Edelman) 1960–61 Law
Wyatt, Thelma L. 1969–70 Law
Wyche, LaMonte G., Sr. 1971–72 Philos.
Yama, Evelyn K. (Kimura) 1953–54
  Social Psychology
Yamaguchi, Donald 1954–56 Medicine
Yamamoto, George K. 1959–60 Sociology
Yamamoto, Hisaye (DeSoto) 1950–51
  Literature
Yasuda, Robert M. 1962–63 Fine Arts
Yee, Robert 1953–54 Political Science
Yellow Robe, Evelyn (Finkbeiner)
  1950–51 Speech
Yoshida, Tadashi 1956–57 Library Sci.
Yoshihashi, T. 1953–54 Int. Relations
Young, Dennis McRay 1970–71 Polit. Sci.
Young, Sandra 1966–67 Mathematics
Zephier, Francine (Dulmage) 1960–61
  Spanish

Appendix B

THE
WHITNEY–FULBRIGHT
PROFESSORS
AND THEIR
HOST INSTITUTIONS

Byung-uk Ahn (Republic of Korea) 1961–62
  Professor of philosophy, Union Christian College, Seoul

Mercer University
Cornell College

Alberto Amador-Sellerier (Mexico) 1961–62
  Coordinator, Art Department, Summer School, and
  professor of architecture, National University of Mexico;
  independent practicing architect

Tulane University
Kent State University

Chun-suk Auh (Republic of Korea) 1962–63
  Professor of education, Ewha Women's
  University, Seoul

MacMurray College
George Peabody College for
Teachers

D'Arco Silvio Avalle (Italy) 1954–55
  Latin language and literature and modern history,
  Instituto Magistrale, Milan

Hamline University and Macalester
College
University of Georgia

Naguib Baladi (Egypt) 1956–57
  Professor of the history of philosophy, faculty of Arts,
  Alexandria University

University of South Dakota
College of Puget Sound

Ronald Burton Ballinger (South Africa) 1961–62
  Senior lecturer (associate professor), in history,
  University of the Witwatersrand

University of Rhode Island
Grinnell College

Onkar Prasad Bhatnager (India) 1958–59
  Reader in history, University of Allahabad

Beloit College
University of Virginia

Izaak J. Brugmans (Netherlands) 1954–55
  Professor of economic history, University of Amsterdam

University of Missouri
Southern Methodist University

Jan Axel Teddy Brunius (Sweden) 1956–57
  Assistant professor of philosophy, University of Uppsala

Grinnell College
Lewis and Clark College

Roberto Caamano (Argentina) 1964–65

Grinnell College

Cesare Cecioni (Italy) 1955–56
  Senior lecturer, English language and literature,
  University of Florence

University of Arkansas
Rollins College

Chen Kuo-hsin (Republic of China) 1964–65
  Professor of political science, National Taiwan
  University, Taipei

St. Joseph College
University of Chattanooga

Pierre Chevrillon (France) 1958–59
  Professor of literature and drama, University of Poitiers

University of Arkansas
Trinity University
University of Utah

Dorothy P. Clarke (North Ireland) 1957–58
  Lecturer in history of the U.S. and British colonial
  history, Queens University, Belfast

Texas Christian University
University of Kentucky

Sven Christian Clausen (Denmark) 1954–55
 Law, political science, and theory of drama,
 University of Copenhagen

University of North Carolina
University of Denver

Simone D'Ardenne (Belgium) 1956–57
 Professor of Anglo-Saxon and Middle English,
 Liege University

Montana State University
University of Alabama

Suram Dasgupta (India) 1957–58
 Reader in philosophy, Lucknow University

University of New Mexico
University of Nebraska

Aloo J. Dastur (India) 1960–61
 Sir Pherozashah Mehta Professor of Politics, Head,
 Department of Politics, University of Bombay

West Virginia University
Valparaiso University

Herbert Stanley Deighton (United Kingdom) 1951–52
 Fellow and dean, modern history, Pembroke College,
 Oxford University

University of New Mexico
Emory University

Carlo M. Della Rocca (Italy) 1959–60
 Professor of Italian language and literature, art, music,
 philosophy, education and psychology,
 Senior High School for Elementary Teachers, Rome

Emory University
Portland State College

Keshubhai Shavjibhai Desai (India) 1963–64
 Reader in political science, University of Baroda,
 Baroda, Gujarat

Hamilton College
Rockford College

Margaret Caldwell Donaldson (Scotland) 1962–63
 Lecturer, developmental psychology, Department of
 Psychology, University of Edinburgh

Southwestern at Memphis
University of Rhode Island

William A. Edwards (Australia) 1951–52
 Head, Department of Modern Languages,
 University of Western Australia, Nedlands

William & Mary College (1st
semester 1951–52)
Reed College (2d semester
1952–53)

Peter Elkin (Australia) 1958–59
 Senior lecturer in English, University of Technology,
 Sydney

Case Institute of Technology
(at their expense)
Wake Forest College

Jorge Elliott-Garcia (Chile) 1957–58
 Professor of literature, University of Concepcion

Lawrence College
University of Oregon

Ake Elmer (Sweden) 1962–63
 Associate professor of social welfare science,
 University of Lund

Denison University
Whitman College

Ahmet Sukru Esmer (Turkey) 1958–59
 Professor of history, University of Ankara

University of Idaho
University of Chattanooga

Thome H. Fang (China) 1959–60
 Professor of Western and Chinese philosophy, Chinese
 Literature and Art, National Taiwan University, Tapei

State University of South Dakota
University of Missouri

Guadalupe Fores-Ganzon (Philippines) 1955–56
 Associate professor of history, College of Liberal Arts,
 University of Philippines, Diliman, Quezon City

Beloit College
New Mexico Highlands University

Rikutaro Fukuda (Japan) 1961–62
 Assistant professor of English and American Literature,
 Tokyo University of Education

Macalester College
Syracuse University

Friedrich Glum (Germany) 1953–54
 Professor of comparative public law and political
 Science, University of Munich

Tulane University
Johns Hopkins University and
Goucher College

Mysore Hatti Gopal (India) 1963–64
 Economics, Member, Railway Rates Tribunal, Madras

Western Maryland College

Cecil Huddlestone Hadgraft (Australia) 1956–57
    Professor of English, University of Queensland

University of Omaha
Louisiana State University

Kissoonsingh Hazareesingh (Mauritius) 1964–65
    Director, Central Information Office,
    Government of Mauritius, Phoenix

Rockford College
Western Maryland College

Josephine Huang Hung (Republic of China) 1963–64
    Professor of western drama, National Taiwan University
    Taipei, Taiwan

Grinnell College
St. Joseph College

K. N. Jayatilleke (Ceylon) 1964–65
    Professor and head of Department of Philosophy,
    University of Ceylon, Peradeniya

University of North Carolina

Mika Kaskimies (Finland) 1959–60
    Professor of economics, Helsinki School of Economics,
    Helsinki

Drake University
University of South Carolina

Heinz S. K. Kent (Australia) 1961–62
    Senior lecturer, international trade relations in the 18th
    century and problems of trade relations in Northern
    Europe, University of Adelaide

Interim 5-week appointment to
lecture at various universities

Edmund James King (England) 1955–56
    Lecturer in comparative education, University of
    London, King's College

Memphis State College

Roberto Koch-Flores (Peru) 1963–64
    Professor at the Faculty of Education,
    National University of San Marcos, Lima

Cornell College
University of Chattanooga

Ineko Kondo (Japan) 1964–65
    Professor of English literature, Tsuda College

University of North Carolina
Rockford College

Leendert Koyck (The Netherlands) 1960–61
    Professor of economics, Netherlands Economic School,
    Rotterdam

Allegheny College
University of Oregon

D. W. Kruger (South Africa) 1962–63
    Professor and head, Department of History, University
    of Potchefstroom

State University College
DePauw University

Jacob P. Kruyt (Netherlands) 1953–54
    Professor of sociology, State University of Utrecht

Howard College
Birmingham Southern College

Laurence D. Lerner (Northern Ireland) 1960–61
    Lecturer in English, Queens University, Belfast

Earlham College
Wofford College
University of Connecticut

Eulalia Maria Lahmeyer Lobo (Brazil) 1960–61
    Instructor of history of the Americas, National Faculty
    of Philosophy, University of Brazil; professor of history,
    Colegio Pedro II (Brazilian Government High School)
    Rio de Janeiro

University of Texas
Occidental College

Zaki N. Mahmoud (Egypt) 1953–54
    Assistant professor of philosophy, University of Cairo

University of South Carolina
State College of Washington

Raghuvansh B. Mathur (India) 1957–58
    Head, Department of Education, Lucknow University

University of Miami
University of Tennessee

Narain Anant Mavlankar (India) 1958–59
    Professor of economics, Fergusson College, Poona

Florida State University
University of Colorado

Jarava Lal Mehta (India) 1964–65
    Reader in philosophy, Central Hindu College,
    Banaras Hindu University, Varanasi

Mount Saint Mary's College

Jose Enrique J. Miguens (Argentina) 1963–64
    Director, Department of Sociology, Catholic University,
    Buenos Aires
      Woman's College of the University
      of North Carolina

Michel Mouskheli (France) 1952–53
    Professor, School of Law, University of Strasbourg
      Vanderbilt and Fisk Universities
      (1 semester)

Sayid Ghulam Mustafa (Pakistan) 1952–53
    Principal, Sind Education Service, Sind Muslim College,
    Karachi
      University of Louisville

George F. K. Naylor (Australia) 1955–56
    Lecturer, philosophy and psychology, University of
    Queensland
      University of Wyoming
      Furman University

Takamichi Ninomiva (Japan) 1960–61
    Professor of English and English literature, Kobe
    University, Tokyo
      Bowdoin College
      Rockford College

Martin Alberto Noel (Argentina) 1959–60
    Professor of Spanish American literature, University
    of Buenos Aires
      Trinity University, San Antonio
      University of Delaware

Ibrahim Noshy (Egypt) 1954–55
    Dean, Faculty of Arts, ancient history and art,
    Ibrahim University, Cairo
      University of North Dakota
      University of Cincinnati

Maria Alice Pessoa (Brazil) 1962–63
    Professor of cultural anthropology and head,
    Department of Fundamental Studies, Brazilian School
    of Public Administration, Rio de Janeiro
      Baldwin-Wallace College
      University of Redlands

Velupillai Raman Pillai (India) 1964–65
    Professor of economics, Kerala University, Trivandrum
      Drake University

Dison Hsueh-feng Poe (Republic of China) 1962–63
    Research Chair Professor, National Chengchi University
      Hanover College
      University of Bridgeport

Ronald V. Sampson (United Kingdom) 1951–52
    Tutor in political theory, Keble College, Oxford
    University
      University of Texas
      University of Colorado

Chandradhar Sharma (India) 1963–64
    Professor and head of Department of Post-Graduate
    Studies and Research in Philosophy, University of
    Jabalpur, Jabalpur
      Gettysburg College
      Hamilton College

Chien-sheng Shih (Republic of China) 1963–64
    Professor and dean, College of Law, National Taiwan
    University, Taipei, Taiwan
      Rockford College
      Mount Saint Mary's College

Bruno K. Suviranta (Finland) 1953–54
    Dean, Faculty of Political Science, Professor of
    Economics, University of Helsinki
      University of Mississippi
      University of Kansas

Ladislao Tarnoi (Venezuela) 1964–65
    Lawyer, Caracas
      Cornell College
      Hamilton College

U Aung Than (Burma) 1961–62
    Professor of Pali, Head, Department of Pali and
    Buddhism, University of Rangoon
      University of Vermont
      Lawrence College

Leslie Wright (Scotland) 1959–60
    Professor of economics, University of Edinburgh
      Rice Institute
      College of William and Mary

Chisaburoh F. Yamada (Japan) 1963–64
    Professor of the history of art, Kyoritsu Women's
    University, Tokyo University of Arts, Tokyo;
    Executive Committee, National Museum of Modern Art
      The Woman's College of the
      University of North Carolina
      Drake University

Kwang-chung Yu (Republic of China) 1964–65
  Professor of Chinese Literature

Gettysburg College

Yahya Kazim Zabunoglu (Turkey) 1964–65
  Assistant of public law, University of Ankara

Drake University

Mohamad M. Ziada (Egypt) 1952–53
  Professor of medieval history and head, History
  Department, Fouad I University, Cairo

University of Florida
University of Utah

Appendix C

THE WHITNEY
VISITING PROFESSORS,
1952–1963

John Alford, 1954–55
Fine arts, R.I. School of Design

Middlebury College*

Horace Alwyne, 1957–58
Music, Bryn Mawr College

Grinnell College*

Gerald Barnes, 1960–61
Sociology, Boston University

Goucher College

Maurice Baudin, 1960–61
French, New York Univ.

Heidelberg College*

Louis Brand, 1956–57
Mathematics, Univ. of Cincinnati

Trinity College, Hartford

Harold Bruce, 1958–59
Government, Dartmouth College

Pomona College†

Paul Burlin, 1954–55
Fine arts, Washington Univ.

Union College

Gladys Campbell, 1957–58
Humanities, Univ. of Chicago

Virginia Union Univ.

Manmatha Chatterjee, 1954–55
Social science, Antioch College

Bennett College

Samuel Clagett Chew, 1954–55
English literature, Bryn Mawr College

Pomona College

Arthur C. Cole, 1956–57
History, Brooklyn College

C. W. Post College

John Collier, 1955–56
Anthropology, City College of New York

Knox College

Cornelia C. Coulter, 1952–53
Classics, Mount Holyoke College

Hiram College

Avery Craven, 1955–56
American history, Univ. of Chicago

Univ. of Richmond Center*

Herbert L. Creek, 1953–54
English, Purdue Univ.

Coe College*

John F. Dashiell, 1958–59
Psychology, Univ. of No. Carolina

Wake Forest College†

* Supported by funds contributed by the New York Foundation
† Supported by funds contributed by The Danforth Foundation

Dorothy W. Dennis, 1959–60   Rockford College
French, Wellesley College

Howard O. Eaton, 1956–57   Shorter College
Philosophy, Univ. of Oklahoma

M. C. Elmer, 1957–58   Western College for Women*
Sociology, Univ. of Pittsburgh

Paul D. Evans, 1958–59   Scripps College
European history, Univ. of Vermont

N. Bryllion Fagin, 1958–59   LeMoyne College†
English, Johns Hopkins Univ.

Ernst Feise, 1953–54   Whittier College
German, Johns Hopkins Univ.

Hilbert T. Ficken, 1952–53   Furman Univ.
German, comp. lit., Baldwin-Wallace College

Harold H. Fisher, 1961–62   Mills College*
History, Stanford Univ.

Martin Foss, 1960–61   Labanon Valley College*
Philosophy, Haverford College

Herman Frankel, 1953–54   Beloit College
Classics, Stanford Univ.

Paul Friedlander, 1953–54   Scripps College*
Classics, Univ. of California

William A. Gaw, 1957–58   Earlham College†
Art, Mills College

Wesley M. Gewehr, 1959–60   Columbia College†
History, Univ. of Maryland

William Chase Greene, 1957–58   Wells College
Greek, Latin, Harvard Univ.

Karl Grossman, 1958–59   California Western Univ.
Music, Western Reserve Univ.

James Husst Hall, 1955–56   Univ. of Richmond Center*
Music, Oberlin College

Clarence Hamilton, 1954–55   Hamilton College*
Philos. of religion, Oberlin College

Hornell Hart, 1957–58   Centre College of Kentucky
Sociology, Duke University

Emil Hauser, 1961–62   Bard College
Music, Bard College

Luike John Hemmes, 1958–59   Simpson College†
Philosophy, religion, Kalamazoo College

Cecilia H. Hendricks, 1953–54   Coe College*
English, Indiana Univ.

Camila Henriquez-Urena, 1959–60   Centre College of Kentucky*
Spanish, Vassar College

Philip M. Hicks, 1954–55   Birmingham-Southern College*
English literature, Swarthmore College

* Supported by funds contributed by the New York Foundation
† Supported by funds contributed by The Danforth Foundation

Howard T. Hill, 1961–62
Speech, Kansas State College

Park College *

Harry M. Hubbell, 1953–54
Greek, Yale Univ.

Goucher College

Jay B. Hubbell, 1955–56
American literature, Duke Univ.

Univ. of Richmond Center

Joseph Hudnut, 1953–54
Architecture, design, Harvard Univ.

Colby College *

Chesley M. Hutchings, 1959–60
Romance language, lit., Univ. of Cincinnati

Hampden-Sydney College *

John Ise, 1955–56
Economics, Univ. of Kansas

Goucher College

Waclaw Jedrzejewicz, 1958–59
Russian, Wellesley College

Ripon College

Claudius O. Johnson, 1960–61
Political science, State College of Washington

Chatham College *

Leo Katz, 1955–56
Art, Hampton Institute

Spelman College

F. Wilhelm Kaufmann, 1958–59
German, Oberlin College

Grinnell College *

Alexander Kelso, 1957–58
Philosophy, Christian ethics, Southwestern at Memphis

Converse College

Lawrence Kinnaird, 1962–63
History, Univ. of California

Chatham College

Paul Knaplund, 1955–56
History, Univ. of Wisconsin

Wells College

Elisabeth Koffka, 1961–62
History, Smith College

Lawrence College *

Hans Kohn, 1962–63
History, City College of New York

Social Science Foundation,
Univ. of Denver

Harry Kurz, 1959–60
Romance languages, Queens College

C. W. Post College *

M. Willard Lampe, 1955–56
Religion, State Univ. of Iowa

Skidmore College *

Howard C. Lane, 1959–60
English, Cornell College

Cornell College, Mt. Vernon, Iowa

Robert Langer, 1960–61
Political science, Queens College

Hofstra College

John P. Le Coq, 1954–55
Romance languages, Drake Univ.

Southwestern at Memphis

Shao Chang Lee, 1960–61
Foreign studies, Michigan State Univ.

Bates College *

William C. Lehman, 1954–55
Sociology, Syracuse Univ.

Center College of Kentucky

Ernest M. Linton, 1953–54
Government, Indiana Univ.

Fisk Univ. *

* Supported by funds contributed by the New York Foundation

C. F. Littell, 1955–56
History, political sci., Cornell College

Hollins College

Andrei Lobanov-Rostovsky, 1961–62
History, Univ. of Michigan

Davidson College*

S. Gale Lowrie, 1955–56
Political science, Univ. of Cincinnati

Rollins College*

Mary McKinney, 1956–57
Classics, Albion College

Austin College

Jeronimo Mallo, 1958–59
Spanish, State Univ. of Iowa

Carleton College†

Erwin K. Mapes, 1952–53
Spanish, State Univ. of Iowa

Kenyon College

Alexander P. Maslow, 1960–61
Philosophy, Univ. of British Columbia

St. Olaf College

Kirtley F. Mather, 1955–56
Geology, Harvard Univ.

Carleton College*

Thomas Means, 1960–61
Greek, Latin, Bowdoin College

Dickinson College

Bruno Meinecke, 1956–57
Classics, Univ. of Michigan

Gettysburg College*

William S. Messer, 1952–53
Latin language, lit., Dartmouth College

Whitman College

Jacob Conrad Meyer
History, Western Reserve Univ.

Spelman College

Charles C. Mierow, 1956–57
Classics, Carleton College

Colorado College*

Broadus Mitchell, 1958–59
Economics, Rutgers Univ.

Hofstra College

Marcel Moraud, 1959–60
French, Rice Institute

Wheaton College†

Clyde Murley, 1955–56
Classical languages, Northwestern Univ.

Univ. of Redlands*

Richard A. Newhall, 1956–57
European history, Williams College

Colby College*

Herman Clarence Nixon, 1956–57
Political science, Vanderbilt Univ.

Whittier College

Filmer S. C. Northrop, 1959–61
Philosophy, law, Yale Univ.

Rollins College†

Frank O'Hara, 1953–54
English, drama, Univ. of Chicago

College of Idaho*

Louise Overacker, 1957–58
Political science, Wellesley College

Bethany College†

Charlotte H. Pekary, 1961–62
German, New York Univ.

Western College for Women*

* Supported by funds contributed by the New York Foundation
† Supported by funds contributed by The Danforth Foundation

Stephen C. Pepper, 1958–59
Philosophy, Univ. of California

Colby College

L. Denis Peterkin, 1954–55
Classics, lit., Harvard Univ.

Dickinson College

Julius W. Pratt, 1958–59
History, Univ. of Buffalo

Hood College*

Hereward T. Price, 1953–54
English, Univ. of Michigan

Lawrence College*

Daniel S. Robinson, 1954–55
Philosophy, Univ. of So. California

Bethany College

Kenneth Robinson, 1959–60
English, Dartmouth College

Birmingham-Southern College†

W. C. Ronan, 1957–58
Architecture, Ohio State Univ.

Thiel College*

Roger D. Rusk, 1958–59
Physics, Mount Holyoke College

Furman University†

Harold St. John, 1958–59
Botany, Univ. of Hawaii

Chatham College*

Helen E. Sandison, 1954–55
English, Vassar College

Washington College*

George Paul Schmidt, 1960–61
History, Douglass College, Rutgers Univ.

Thiel College*

Herbert W. Schneider, 1958–59
Philos., religion, Columbia Univ.

Colorado College*

Paul Schrecker, 1961–62
Philosophy, Univ. of Pennsylvania

Claremont Graduate School

Robert L. Schuyler, 1953–54
History, Columbia Univ.

Hobard and William Smith
Colleges

Laurens H. Seelye, 1959–60
Philosophy, Robert College (Istanbul)

Rollins College*

William E. Shideler, 1957–58
Geology, Miami Univ.

Hiram College

Orrin H. Smith, 1957–58
Physics, DePauw Univ.

Kalamazoo College†

Wilbert Snow, 1954–55
English literature, Wesleyan Univ.

Morehouse College*

George Soule, 1958–59
Economics, Bennington College

Washington College,
Chestertown, Md.

Walter Terence Stace, 1955–56
Philosophy, Princeton Univ.

Wheaton College

Boris M. Stanfield, 1957–58
Economics, Columbia Univ.

Hobart and William Smith
Colleges*

Dorothy Stimson, 1957–58
History, Goucher College

Sarah Lawrence College*

* Supported by funds contributed by the New York Foundation
† Supported by funds contributed by The Danforth Foundation

Mary E. Storer, 1955–56
French, Beloit College

Allegheny College

Harvey Stork, 1957–58
Botany, Carleton College

Tougaloo Southern College

Robert Parvin Strickler, 1956–57
Greek, Southwestern at Memphis

Bard College

Jane J. Swenarton, 1955–56
English, Vassar College

Wilson College*

Emerson H. Swift, 1958–59
Fine arts, Columbia Univ.

Southwestern at Memphis

Donald R. Taft, 1956–57
Sociology, anthropol., Univ. of Illinois

Dillard University

Vivian Trow Thayer, 1956–57
Education, Univ. of Virginia

Fisk University*

A. Pelzer Wagener, 1959–60
Ancient languages, College of William and Mary

Austin College†

Eda Lou Walton, 1960–61
English, New York Univ.

Bennett College†

Clarence Ward, 1953–54
Fine arts, Oberlin College

Univ. of the South

Samuel M. Waxman, 1956–57
Romance languages, Boston Univ.

Union College*

Thomas J. Wertenbaker, 1957–58
History, Princeton Univ.

Hampden-Sydney College†

Robert C. Whitford, 1957–58
English, Pratt Institute

Wilson College

Kossuth M. Williamson, 1959–60
Economics, social sci., Wesleyan Univ.

Wilkes College*

James S. Wilson, 1953–54
English, Univ. of Virginia

Davidson College

Louis Wolferz, 1952–53
French, German, Yenching Univ. (China)

Earlham College

Arthur Evans Wood, 1952–53
Sociology, Univ. of Michigan

Wittenberg College

Leavitt O. Wright, 1960–61
Romance languages, Univ. of Oregon

Claremont Men's College*

* Supported by funds contributed by the New York Foundation
† Supported by funds contributed by The Danforth Foundation